Mark Edward Soper

Sams **Teach Yourself**

Windows 7

in **10 Minutes**

SAMS | 800 East 96th Street, Indianapolis, Indiana 46240

Sams Teach Yourself Windows 7 in 10 Minutes

Copyright © 2011 by Pearson Education, Inc.

Library of Congress Cataloging-in-Publication data is on file.

Printed in the United States of America

First Printing September 2010

Trademarks

All terms mentioned in this book that are known to be trademarks or service marks have been appropriately capitalized. Pearson Education, Inc. cannot attest to the accuracy of this information. Use of a term in this book should not be regarded as affecting the validity of any trademark or service mark.

Warning and Disclaimer

Bulk Sales

Pearson Education, Inc. offers excellent discounts on this book when ordered in quantity for bulk purchases or special sales. For more information, please contact

U.S. Corporate and Government Sales
1-800-382-3419
corpsales@pearsontechgroup.com

For sales outside of the U.S., please contact

International Sales
international@pearson.com

ISBN-13: 978-0-67233328-6

ISBN-10: 0-672-33328-7

Associate Publisher
Greg Wiegand

Acquisitions Editor
Rick Kughen

Development Editors
Michael Henry
and
Rick Kughen

Managing Editor
Kristy Hart

Project Editors
Jovana San Nicolas-Shirley
and Kelly Craig

Copy Editor
Apostrophe Editing Services

Indexer
Erika Millen

Technical Editor
Mark Reddin

Publishing Coordinator
Cindy Teeters

Book Designer
Anne Jones

Compositor
Nonie Ratcliff

Contents at a Glance

Table of Contents

About the Author

Mark Edward Soper is the author or coauthor of more than 20 books on technology topics, including two books on Windows Vista, one previous book on Windows 7, and many print and online articles on Windows Vista and Windows 7 for *Maximum PC* print and online editions and InformIT.com. Mark has also contributed to *Special Edition Using* and *In Depth* books on Windows versions from Me and XP through Windows 7 and has also written and coauthored three A+ Certification books. Mark also has 20 years of consumer and corporate training experience in Windows, application software, networking, and hardware upgrading and repair.

Dedication

For Felix—welcome to the family!

Acknowledgments

A book is a partnership of many, and I want to thank those who made this book possible.

First, I thank God for the opportunity to share the adventure of learning more about technology with you, my readers. Your support makes this and other books possible.

Next, my family rates a big "thank you" for listening patiently (not to mention smiling and nodding) as the family geeks discuss, debate, and dissect computers and related technologies. I want to especially thank Jeremy for performing screen captures for several chapters.

A big "thank you" also goes out to Microsoft Corporation for listening to what real people want to do with their computers, getting hardware and software vendors to take Windows 7 seriously, and producing an outstanding operating system that's a pleasure to use—and write about.

Finally, many thanks to the people at Pearson Education, the parent company of Que Publishing, including

Rick Kughen, who continues to be a pleasure to work with from start to finish; Greg Wiegand, who gave the go-ahead for this project; Michael Henry, for keeping the development of this book running along; Jovana San Nicolas-Shirley, for keeping a careful eye on the different pieces of this book; Mark Reddin, for helping squash any technical glitches that might arise; Cindy Teeters, for keeping those payments coming; Anne Jones, for making this book a pleasure to view and use; and the rest of the team, who continue to produce the industry's best technology books.

We Want to Hear from You!

As the reader of this book, *you* are our most important critic and commentator. We value your opinion and want to know what we're doing right, what we could do better, what areas you'd like to see us publish in, and any other words of wisdom you're willing to pass our way.

You can email or write me directly to let me know what you did or didn't like about this book—as well as what we can do to make our books stronger.

Please note that I cannot help you with technical problems related to the topic of this book and that due to the high volume of mail I receive, I might not be able to reply to every message.

When you write, please be sure to include this book's title and author as well as your name and phone or email address. I will carefully review your comments and share them with the author and editors who worked on the book.

E-mail: consumer@samspublishing.com

Mail: Greg Wiegand
Associate Publisher
Sams Publishing
800 East 96th Street
Indianapolis, IN 46240 USA

Reader Services

Visit our website and register this book at informit.com/register for convenient access to any updates, downloads, or errata that might be available for this book.

Introduction

How to Use This Book

Most PC users have encountered some version of Windows previously but find a lot that's new in Windows 7. If that describes you, this is the book for you, especially if you don't have a lot of spare time on your hands. Make those 10-minute time chunks you can devote to learning more about Windows 7 useful and enjoyable with Teach Yourself Windows 7 in 10 Minutes. Here's why:

▶ We don't waste your time teaching you stuff about Windows 7 that's the same as in previous versions.

▶ We don't waste your time discussing why Windows 7 does what it does.

▶ We do make the most of your time by teaching you the major new features in Windows 7 concisely and accurately with a liberal use of figures and step-by-step instructions.

With this goal in mind, what's the best way for you to use this book? As you use Windows 7, use the following chapter synopses (and the everhelpful Table of Contents) to look up features you need help mastering. Turn to those sections, try the exercises, and you'll improve your mastery of Windows 7.

What's Inside the Book?

Teach Yourself Windows 7 in Ten Minutes contains eleven chapters. Here's what you'll find.

▶ Lesson 1, "Getting Started with Windows 7," teaches you how to log into Windows 7, how to use and manage the new Start menu, run programs from the Start menu, use Instant Desktop Search, make and use a password reset disk, use jump lists to start frequently-used files and tasks for your favorite programs from the Start menu, and shut down or hibernate your computer.

▶ Lesson 2, "Managing Your Desktop," shows you how to use new features in the taskbar, such as jump lists and live previews; create a theme that stores your preferred desktop background, window color, screen saver, and event sounds for easy recall and reuse; tweak your screen resolution to get the best view from today's high-res displays; configure an external display on a laptop or a second monitor on a desktop; and add small programs (gadgets) to your display and customize them.

▶ Lesson 3, "Working with Libraries," brings you up to speed on one of Windows 7's most innovative new features: the ability to put all the folders where you store documents, photos, music, and videos into a single, logical folder called a library. Libraries make finding files easy, backups easier to set up, and also provide new and improved ways to see more information about a particular file.

▶ Lesson 4, "Enjoying Photos and Media," introduces you to the new Windows Photo Viewer, enhanced Print Pictures Wizard, improved features in Windows Media Player, and teaches you how to play media with Windows Media Center.

▶ Lesson 5, "Managing Devices and Printers," helps you master the new Devices and Printers management interface for your computer's built-in and add-on hardware and new Device Stage drivers for multifunction devices such as all-in-one units and smartphones.

▶ Lesson 6, "Connecting to a Wireless Network," teaches you how to connect to a wireless network and manage your connections the new Windows 7 way.

▶ Lesson 7, "Browsing the Web Faster and More Securely with IE8," helps you start and tweak Windows 7's default web browser, handle pages that don't display properly, use the enhanced website history feature to get to your favorite sites faster, keep your browsing confidential with InPrivate, view multiple pages in one browser window with tabs, and store multiple tabs as a single favorite.

▶ Lesson 8, "Creating and Using a Homegroup," brings you up to speed on how to create a secure and easy-to-manage homegroup network among your Windows 7 computers.

▶ Lesson 9, "Connecting to Other Windows Computers," helps you add your new Windows 7 computer to an existing network containing computers running Windows XP or Windows Vista, access shared folders, and print to shared printers.

▶ Lesson 10, "Using Windows Backup," shows you how to make a backup of your system and files you can use to recover from a disaster, keep it updated with scheduled backups, create a system repair disc you can use for disaster recovery, and test your backup to be sure it works.

▶ Lesson 11, "Using Action Center," helps you master this new feature for reporting system security and maintenance problems and helps you troubleshoot problems with your system.

By teaching you the essentials of Windows 7 in a simple, no-frills manner, Teach Yourself Windows 7 in 10 Minutes helps make Windows 7 more useful and more fun with a minimal time commitment from you.

Conventions Used in This Book

Whenever you need to click a particular button or link in Windows or one of the other sites described in this book, you'll find the label or name for that item bolded in the text, such as "Click the **Create an Account** button." In addition to the text and figures in this book, you also encounter some special boxes labelled Tip, Note, or Caution.

TIP: Tips offer helpful shortcuts or easier ways to do something.

NOTE: Notes are extra bits of information related to the text that might help you expand your knowledge or understanding.

CAUTION: Cautions are warnings or other important information you need to know about the consequences of using a feature or executing a task.

LESSON 1

Getting Started with Windows 7

Logging In to Windows 7

Windows 7 is Microsoft's best desktop operating system yet, and the differences start at login time. Whether you installed Windows 7 yourself or use a preinstalled version, you were prompted to create a username and password for each user at first startup. Here's where you put them to work.

After you turn on your computer, the Windows 7 Logon menu appears (Figure 1.1). Click your name or icon to start.

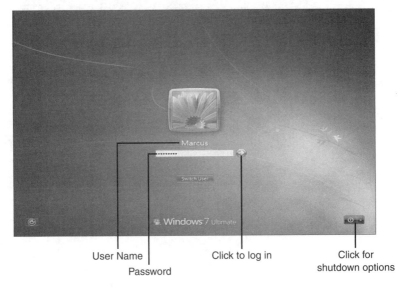

User Name | Click to log in | Click for
Password | | shutdown options

FIGURE 1.1   Logging in to Windows 7.

If you set up a password for the account, type it in and click the right arrow icon to log in to Windows. If there's no password on the account, just click the right arrow.

What if you forget your password? Click **OK** (see Figure 1.2).

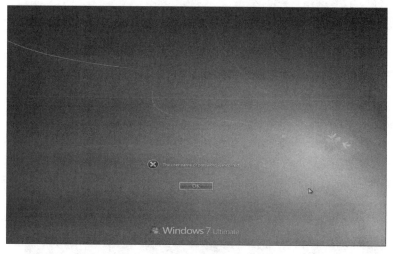

FIGURE 1.2   Mistype password? Forget password? Click OK to see a password hint.

Review the password hint (see Figure 1.3) and enter your password again.

TIP: If you cannot remember your password, you can use the Password Reset Disk (if you have created one) to start your computer. See the sections about creating and using the disk later in this lesson.

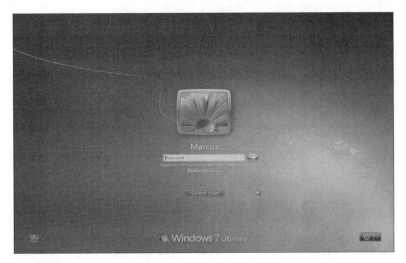

FIGURE 1.3   Windows 7 throws you a password hint if you forget your password.

Using the Start Menu

When the Windows 7 desktop opens, the differences between 7 and its predecessors just keep on coming. Click the "Microsoft marble" (also known as the *Start orb*) to open the Start menu.

The Start menu's left pane displays a list of recently used programs. When you run a program, Windows 7 adds the program shortcut to the list in the left pane. The right pane is the gateway to your folders, the computer's disk drives and other features, hardware settings, default programs, and help (see Figure 1.4).

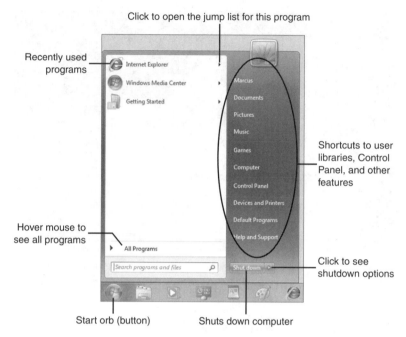

FIGURE 1.4   Clicking the Start orb opens Windows 7's new and improved Start menu.

To access other programs from the Start menu:

1. Hover your mouse over **All Programs**.

2. The left pane transforms into a scrolling list of programs installed with Windows 7 and programs installed later (see Figure 1.5).

3. To return to your original left pane, click **Back**.

FIGURE 1.5   All Programs provides links to programs and folders with still more program shortcuts.

Running Programs from the Start Menu

To start a program from the left pane or a task from the right pane, click the appropriate shortcut (see Figure 1.6).

If you want to start a program after opening **All Programs**, you might need to scroll down to the folder that contains the program you want to run. Click the folder to open it and click the shortcut to run the program (see Figure 1.7).

FIGURE 1.6   Starting Windows DVD Maker.

FIGURE 1.7   Starting Windows Calculator from the Accessories folder.

Managing the Start Menu

Most programs add themselves to the Start menu's list of frequently used programs after you run them for the first time. This is handy if you want to use the program frequently. However, if you don't want the program cluttering up your menu, right-click the program shortcut and select **Remove from This List** (see Figure 1.8). You can also use the right-click menu to place (or "pin") programs to the Taskbar or Start menu.

FIGURE 1.8   Preparing to remove Windows DVD Maker from the Start menu's list of frequently used programs.

To adjust what programs are displayed in the Start menu:

1. In the right pane of the Start menu, right-click the **Start** orb and select **Properties** (see Figure 1.9).

2. Click the **Customize** button on the Start Menu tab (see Figure 1.10).

FIGURE 1.9   Opening the Properties sheet for the Start menu, taskbar, and toolbars.

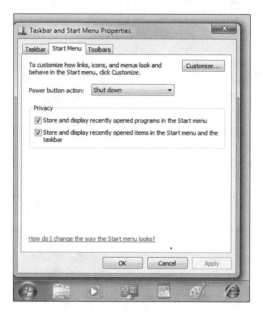

FIGURE 1.10   Preparing to customize the Start menu.

3. Scroll down the list and click/clear check boxes to enable or disable items.

4. Click radio buttons as needed to change how items display.

5. Click **OK** when finished (see Figure 1.11) and then **Apply** and **OK** on the Start Menu tab (refer to Figure 1.10) to save your changes.

Figures 1.12 and 1.13 compare the appearance of the Start menu when using defaults and after adding some items.

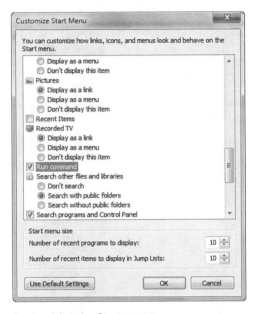

FIGURE 1.11   Customizing the Start menu.

FIGURE 1.12   Default right pane of the Start menu.

FIGURE 1.13   Modified Start menu right pane after adding Homegroup, Run, Recorded TV, and Network shortcuts.

Searching for Files and Programs

Windows 7 includes an improved version of the Instant Desktop Search feature first included in Windows Vista. To search for a file or program:

1. Enter the first few letters of the filename or program name (see Figure 1.14).

FIGURE 1.14   Using Instant Desktop Search to find a file or program.

2. As you type additional letters, the list becomes shorter in size (see Figure 1.15).

3. When the file or program you want to open displays, click it with your mouse to open it.

Text match in Windows
features that ———
can be turned off

Text match in
program name

Search text ———

FIGURE 1.15   Narrowing down the search by entering more of the file or program name.

Using Search to Help Create a Password Reset Disk

The ability to search by name saves a lot of time when you want to perform a particular task. For example, Windows 7 enables you to create a password reset disk but does not list this program on the Start menu or in Control Panel.

> NOTE: Creating a Password Reset Disk enables you to start your computer, even if you forget your password. You must know your current password to use this feature.

To run the Password Reset Disk program:

1. Enter **password reset** into the search text box (see Figure 1.16).

FIGURE 1.16   Finding the password reset disk program by using Search.

2. Click **Create a Password Reset Disk**.

3. The Welcome dialog appears (see Figure 1.17).

4. Insert your preferred media (USB flash drive, flash memory card, or floppy disk) before clicking **Next**.

5. Select the location for the reset disk (you can use a floppy disk, a USB flash memory drive, or a flash memory card) and click **Next** (see Figure 1.18).

FIGURE 1.17   Starting the Forgotten Password Wizard.

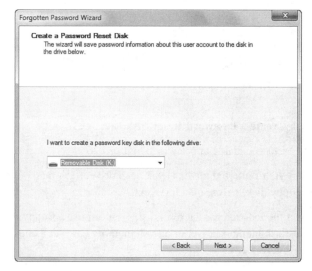

FIGURE 1.18   Selecting a drive to use for the reset disk.

6. Enter the password for the current user and click **Next** (see Figure 1.19). To protect your privacy, dots appear as you enter your password.

FIGURE 1.19   Entering the current password.

7. The wizard writes the password to the disk or flash drive.

8. When the process is complete, click **Next**. Remove the media, label it, and click **Finish**.

Using the Password Reset Disk

If you forget your password when you try to log in to Windows 7 in the future, here's how to use the Password Reset Disk to log into your system:

1. Click the **Reset Password** link (refer to Figure 1.3) to start the Password Reset Wizard.

2. From the opening dialog (see Figure 1.20), click **Next** to continue.

3. Insert the password reset disk or flash drive and select the correct drive letter when prompted. Click **Next** to continue (see Figure 1.21).

FIGURE 1.20   Starting the Password Reset Wizard.

FIGURE 1.21   Specifying the password reset disk location.

4. Enter a new password, re-enter it, and type a new password hint when prompted. Click **Next** to continue (see Figure 1.22).

FIGURE 1.22   Specifying a new password and password hint.

5. Click **Finish** to complete the wizard.

> NOTE: You can use the same reset disk repeatedly if you forget your password, so be sure to keep it safe.

Working with Jump Lists

Windows 7 automatically creates a list of recently opened files and tasks for each program in its frequently used list. This list is called a *jump list*. To figure out whether a program has a jump list, look for a right arrow next to the program listing in the Start menu (refer to Figure 1.4). To open the jump list, click the right arrow.

Some items in Windows 7's Start menu include a jump list by default, such as Getting Started, a collection of programs useful for setting up Windows 7. Figure 1.23 shows the jump list for Getting Started.

NOTE: In programs such as Microsoft Word or other parts of Microsoft Office, the contents of the jump list correspond to the list of recently used files on the File menu.

FIGURE 1.23   Viewing the jump list for Getting Started.

Jump lists save you time by enabling you to go directly to the task you want to perform. If you prefer, you can also open the main program and select the task you want to perform.

Jump lists aren't just for tasks. Jump lists also store shortcuts to frequently opened files. Figure 1.24 illustrates a jump list Windows 7 created from the Internet TV, recorded TV, photo folders, and other content I've viewed recently with Windows Media Center and the TV program guide task I use frequently.

FIGURE 1.24   Windows 7 creates a jump list from frequently used files or tasks you perform with a particular program.

Pinning/Unpinning Items on the Jump List

By default, Windows 7 changes the contents of the Frequent (last-used files) portion of a jump list as you open additional files. (By default, a jump list can contain up to 10 items.)

However, you might want to keep a particular file on the jump list, regardless of whatever else you open. To do this, highlight the filename and click the Pushpin icon (see Figure 1.25). Windows 7 then creates a new category called Pinned (see Figure 1.26).

Click to pin item to the jump list

FIGURE 1.25   Pinning a file to Windows Media Center's jump list.

FIGURE 1.26   Pinning a file to a jump list sets up a new category: Pinned.

If you decide that you don't need the file pinned to the jump list, highlight the filename and click the Pushpin icon again (see Figure 1.27).

FIGURE 1.27   Unpinning a file from Windows Media Center's jump list.

Other Jump List Options

To see other options, right-click a filename on a jump list. Depending on the program and the file, you can choose from these options:

- ▶ Copy
- ▶ Pin to this list
- ▶ Remove from this list

Some jump lists might also include the following (see Figure 1.28) for some or all items:

- ▶ Play with (program name)
- ▶ Properties

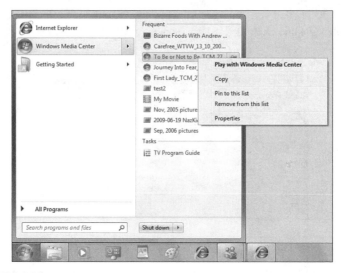

FIGURE 1.28   Additional options for files on a jump list.

Shut Down and Other Options

When it's time to wrap up your work, you can shut down your computer by clicking the **Start** button and clicking **Shut Down**, but for more options, click the right arrow next to Shut Down (see Figure 1.29).

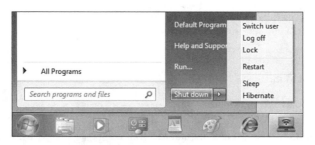

FIGURE 1.29   Shut Down and other options.

These include

▶ **Switch User**—Select this option if more than one user is set up
on your computer and you want another user to run Windows
without logging off Windows yourself. Choosing this option
brings up the login dialog shown in Figure 1.30.

Click to return to original logged-on user

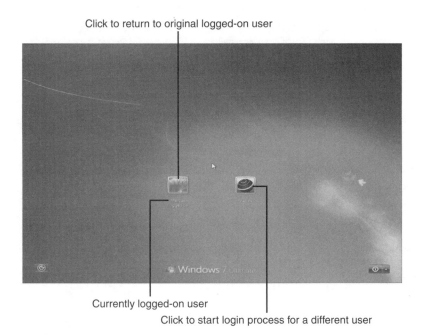

Currently logged-on user

Click to start login process for a different user

FIGURE 1.30   Switching users.

▶ **Log Off**—Logs off the current user and redisplays the login
dialog.

▶ **Lock**—Secures your computer; you must log back in again when
you return.

▶ **Restart**—Restarts your computer; some changes to Windows settings or hardware installations might require a restart.

▶ **Sleep**—Puts computer into a low-power mode, which is useful for keeping programs open so you can restart work quickly.

▶ **Hibernate**—Saves current computer state (open programs, windows, files) to a special system file called hiberfil.sys and then shuts down computer. Useful when you must stop work in one location with a mobile computer and want to go back to what you were doing later. Also works with desktop computers.

CAUTION: Some computers might take a long time to return from sleep or hibernate modes. In some cases, upgrading driver files can improve how quickly the computer can return from these modes.

LESSON 2

Managing Your Desktop

Working with the Taskbar and Jump Lists

Windows 7's taskbar can do much more than in previous versions of Windows. When you start a program with Windows 7, it places an icon for that program on the taskbar. You can also place icons on the taskbar to provide shortcuts to programs not currently running to make them easier to launch. An icon on the taskbar with a box around it indicates that the program is currently running.

When you start a program, it is automatically added to the taskbar. To keep the program on the taskbar, right-click the program icon and select **Pin This Program to Taskbar**.

To get more information about a program that's running, hover your mouse over the icon to display a live thumbnail. If you see more than one thumbnail, you have more than one program window open.

Figure 2.1 illustrates these features of the Windows 7 taskbar.

Windows 7 automatically creates a list of recently opened files, websites, or tasks for each program. To see this list, right-click an icon in the taskbar. This list is called a *jump list* because you can jump immediately to the file, website, or tasks by selecting it. Figure 2.2 displays examples of jump lists for Windows utilities.

- ► Websites or folder locations that you have opened frequently display in the **Frequent** part of the jump list.

- ► Files that you have opened recently display in the **Recent** part of the jump list.

- ► Tasks that you can start display in the **Tasks** part of the jump list.

Thumbnail for selected program window

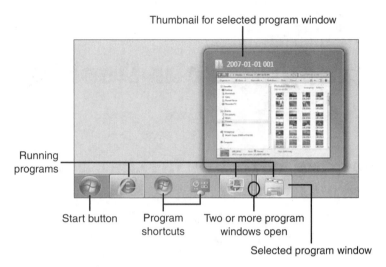

Running programs

Start button   Program shortcuts   Two or more program windows open

Selected program window

FIGURE 2.1   Program icons on the Windows 7 taskbar.

Recently created files

Files which will stay on jump list until unpinned

Frequently viewed or opened files and folders

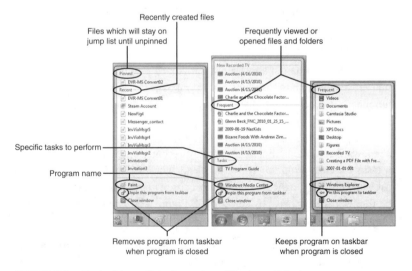

Specific tasks to perform

Program name

Removes program from taskbar when program is closed

Keeps program on taskbar when program is closed

FIGURE 2.2   Typical jump lists for various Windows 7 features.

Windows 7 automatically manages the **Frequent** and **Recent** entries on the jump list. By pinning an item (which places the item into the Pinned section of a jump list as in Figure 2.2), you can access the item at any time, no matter how many other items you have opened or used in the meantime.

Here's how to pin an item to the jump list:

1. Highlight an entry in the Frequent or Recent list.

2. Right-click the entry.

3. Select **Pin to This List** (see Figure 2.3).

Right-click to open options for item

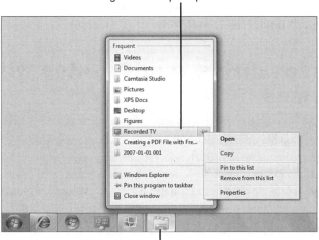

Right-click to open jump list

FIGURE 2.3   Preparing to pin an item to the jump list.

4. If you no longer need access to the item, hover your mouse over the item, click the Pin icon, and the item will be unpinned from the list.

Here's how to add a program to the taskbar:

1. Open the Start menu and scroll to the program you want to add or locate the program shortcut on the Windows desktop.

2. Right-click the program name or program shortcut.

3. Select **Pin to Taskbar**.

> NOTE: You can also drag a program shortcut from the Start menu or the Windows desktop to the taskbar.

To unpin an icon from the taskbar:

1. Right-click the icon

2. Select **Unpin from Taskbar**.

Many programs on the Start menu also maintain a jump list. (Refer to Lesson 1, "Getting Started with Windows 7," for details.)

Personalizing Your Desktop with Themes

Although the standard Windows 7 desktop features a background (wallpaper) based on the new Windows packaging, chances are you'd prefer your own desktop background. To change your desktop background and other settings, right-click an empty section of the desktop and select **Personalize**. In the Personalization menu you can change four settings: desktop background, window color, sounds, and screen saver.

By selecting a theme, you can change the desktop background, window color, event sounds, and screen saver at the same time. Standard options (see Figure 2.4) include

- ▶ **Aero Themes**—Designed to take full advantage of the Aero desktop and include the default Windows 7 theme, architecture, characters, landscapes, nature, and United States. All except the Windows 7 theme use a slideshow with changing images for your desktop background (wallpaper).

▶ **Basic and High Contrast Themes**—Includes a basic theme for
Windows 7, a Windows classic theme reminiscent of an earlier
versions of Windows, and four high-contrast schemes designed
for use by people with visual impairments.

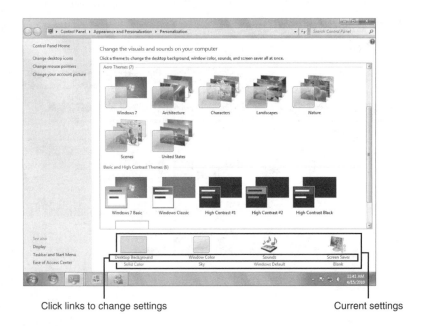

Click links to change settings   Current settings

FIGURE 2.4   Viewing standard themes.

To use a new theme, click the theme you want to use; then close the dialog. The settings take effect immediately.

You can also change the elements of a theme separately and save the
results as a new theme.

Changing the Desktop Background

To change only the desktop background, click the **Desktop Background**
link at the bottom of the Personalization window (refer to Figure 2.4).

The default selections include all photographs in the architecture, characters, landscapes, nature, scenes, United States themes, and the standard Windows 7 background. However, you can also select from several other types of backgrounds. To choose other types of backgrounds, open the picture location menu at the top of the Choose Your Desktop Background dialog (see Figure 2.5).

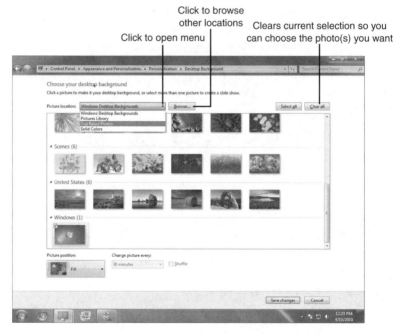

FIGURE 2.5   Choosing a desktop background.

Other options for pictures include your pictures library, top-rated photos, and solid colors. By default, all photos in the pictures library, top-rated photos, and Windows desktop backgrounds are selected. If you want to use only a single photo or a selection of photos for your background, click the **Clear All** button at the upper-right corner of the desktop background dialog. Then, to choose a single background, click the image. If you want to choose from multiple backgrounds, click the first background, hold down the control key, and click any additional backgrounds you want to use as part of a slideshow.

In addition to selecting the image that you want for your background, you can also change three options at the bottom of the dialog: **Picture Position**, **Change Picture Timing**, and **Shuffle**.

To set up these options for your picture background:

1. Open the picture position menu (defaults to Full).

2. Select from **Stretch Picture**, **Tile the Picture**, or **Center the Picture** (see Figure 2.6).

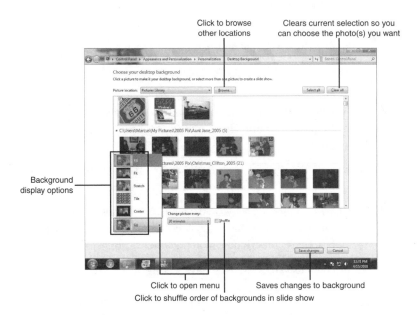

FIGURE 2.6   Selecting the position of the background on the desktop.

3. If you have selected more than one picture, open the **Change Picture Every** menu).

4. Select the interval between picture changes (options range from as little as 10 seconds to as long as 1 day).

5. If you want to view photos in random order, click the empty **Shuffle** check box.

6. To save changes, click the **Save Changes** button.

> NOTE: When you select individual photographs rather than an entire theme, the desktop background is identified as Slideshow.

Changing Window Color

You can change the default window color to your choice of pre-set colors or a custom color. To change the window color:

1. Click the **Window Color** link in the Personalization menu to open the **Window Color and Appearance** menu.

2. Choose a color from the menu.

3. If you're not satisfied with the default color selections, click the **Show Color Mixture** menu and choose a customized color by adjusting the **Hue**, **Saturation**, and **Brightness** sliders (see Figure 2.7).

4. By default, the edges of the window are transparent. To make the window opaque, clear the **Enable Transparency** check box.

5. To adjust the color intensity, adjust the **Color Intensity** slider to the left to make the window less intense (more transparent) or to the right to make the window more intense (less transparent).

6. To save and use changes, click **Save Changes**.

Although the Window Color and Appearance menu has a link called Advanced Appearance Settings, you can disregard this link because the changes you make take effect only if you use the Windows basic or high contrast themes (refer to in Figure 2.1). If you select one of these themes and click **Window Color**, the Window Color and Appearance dialog shown in Figure 2.8 opens. Select the item you want to change, such as the desktop, 3D objects, hyperlinks, menus, scrollbars, and many others, and then choose relevant options such as size, colors, fonts, font sizes, font color, and text attributes. To put changes into effect, click **Apply**; then click **OK**.

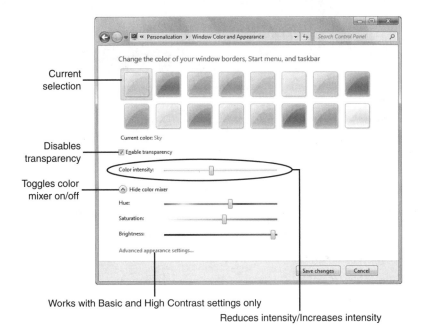

FIGURE 2.7   The Window Color and Appearance menu for Aero themes.

Changing Sounds

Windows 7 themes employ sounds for different events, including errors starting Windows, closing windows, opening windows, and many others. Each theme has a sound scheme associated with it (Windows 7 includes more than a dozen sound schemes), but you can select from many other sound schemes, modify a sound scheme, or even disable sound schemes altogether.

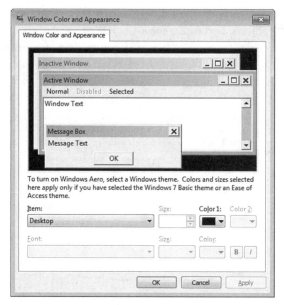

FIGURE 2.8 The Window Color and Appearance menu for Windows basic and high contrast (Ease of Access) themes.

To preview or adjust sound scheme settings:

▶ Click the **Sounds** link at the bottom of the Personalization menu (refer to Figure 2.4).

▶ Choose a scheme from the Sound Scheme menu.

> TIP: The sound used for the event is shown at the bottom of the Sound dialog.

▶ To preview the sound, select any event with a Speaker icon next to it.

▶ To hear the sound, click the **Test** button (see Figure 2.9).

▶ To change the sound or to assign a sound to an event that doesn't currently have a sound, click the **Browse** button.

Click to select sound scheme

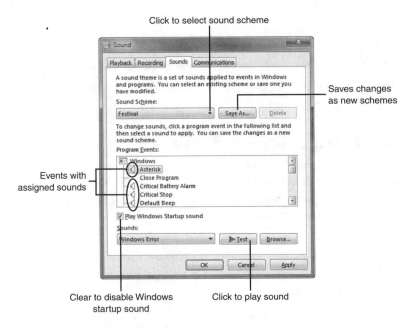

Saves changes
as new schemes

Events with
assigned sounds

Clear to disable Windows   Click to play sound
startup sound

FIGURE 2.9   Working with sound schemes.

NOTE: By default, Windows uses WAV sounds stored in a Media
folder. You can select any sound in this folder or its subfolder for
an event or any other WAV sound on your system.

▶ Navigate to the folder containing the sound.

▶ Highlight a sound and click **Open** to use the selected sound.

If you add sounds to an event, change the sound already assigned to an
event, or remove assigned sounds from an event, you have modified an
existing sound scheme.

To disable the startup sound only, clear the **Play Windows Startup Sound**
check box. To disable all events sounds, choose **No Sounds** from the
sound scheme menu.

To save the scheme:

1. Click **Save As**.

2. Provide a name when prompted.

3. Click **OK**.

To start using your changes immediately, click **Apply** after step 2; then click **OK**.

Choosing a Screen Saver

Although Windows 7 includes a number of screen savers, by default, none of the themes in Windows 7 have a screen saver already select. To select a screen saver, click the **Screen Saver** link at the bottom of the Personalization menu (refer to Figure 2.4).

You can choose from more than half a dozen different screen savers installed with Windows 7; if you install Windows Live Photo Gallery (part of Windows Live Essentials), you can select an additional screen saver. To select a screen saver:

1. Open the **Screen Saver** pull-down menu in the Screen Savers Settings dialog, as shown in Figure 2.10.

2. Choose a screen saver from those listed.

3. To use the selected screen saver immediately, click **Apply**.

4. Click **OK** to save any changes you make to screen saver settings.

Options available for a screen saver vary by selected screen saver. (Most have no options.) With all screen savers, you can adjust the amount of time before the screen saver starts with the Wait menu; the options range from as little as one minute to thousands of minutes. To keep your computer secure while the screen saver runs, click the **On Resume Display Login Screen** check box. By enabling this option, you must log back in to Windows 7 after the screen saver starts.

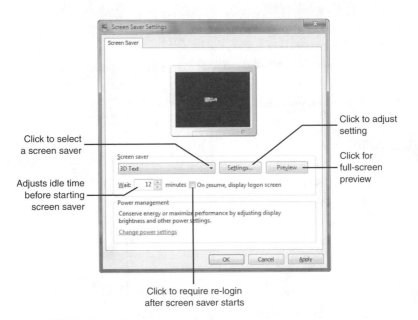

Click to select
a screen saver

Adjusts idle time
before starting
screen saver

Click to adjust
setting

Click for
full-screen
preview

Click to require re-login
after screen saver starts

FIGURE 2.10   Selecting a screen saver.

If you prefer to blank your screen after a particular length of idle time, follow these steps:

1. Click the **Change Power Settings** link shown in Figure 2.10.

2. On the Power Settings dialog, click the **Change Plan Settings**
   link next to the plan you want to change.

3. Adjust the **Turn Off the Display** time as desired (see Figure
   2.11).

4. Click **Save Changes**.

5. Close the Edit Plan Settings dialog and close the Power Settings
   dialog to return to the Screen Saver Settings dialog.

6. Click **Apply**; then click **OK** to save and use changes in settings.

Click to choose settings

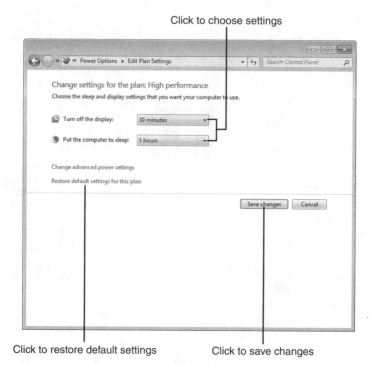

Click to restore default settings   Click to save changes

FIGURE 2.11   Saving changes to a power plan.

Saving a New Theme

If you have made changes to the desktop background, window color, sounds, or screen saver, you have created a new theme. These themes display at the top of the personalization scrolling window in the My Themes section. Until you save it, your modified theme is called "Unsaved Theme."

To save your theme for use by yourself only:

1. Right-click the theme and select **Save Theme** (see Figure 2.12).

2. Enter a name for the theme when prompted.

3. Click **Save**.

Saves theme for your use only

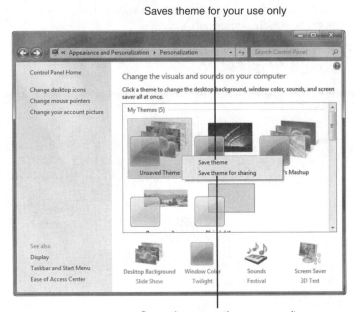

Saves theme so others can use it

FIGURE 2.12   Saving a theme.

If you want other users of this computer to use your theme, right-click the theme and select **Save Theme for Sharing**. A dialog appears enabling you to save the theme into any location you prefer; you can save it to a local or network folder.

After you save the theme, it appears in the My Themes section with the name that you provided. To complete the process of personalizing your desktop, close the Personalization menu.

Adjusting Screen Resolution

Windows 7 makes it easier than ever to select the best screen resolution for your display.

1. Right-click an empty part of the Windows desktop.

2. Select **Screen Resolution**.

3. To determine if the resolution for your display is the best one, open the **Resolution** menu.

4. If the resolution slider is already set to the recommended resolution, everything's fine.

5. If not (see Figure 2.13), move the slider to the recommended resolution.

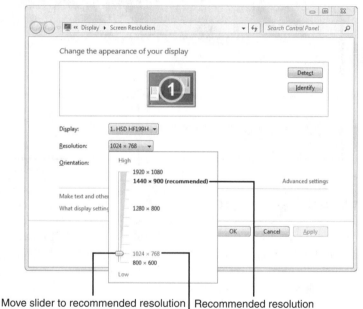

Move slider to recommended resolution | Recommended resolution
Current resolution

FIGURE 2.13   Adjusting your display's resolution.

6. Click **Apply**.

7. Click **OK**.

Configuring Additional Displays

To configure an additional display, make sure the additional display is connected to your computer and turned on. To continue:

1. Open the **Resolution** menu, as shown in Figure 2.13.

2. Click **Detect**. An icon for the additional display appears.

3. Open the **Multiple Displays** menu (see Figure 2.14) and select how you would like to use the additional display:

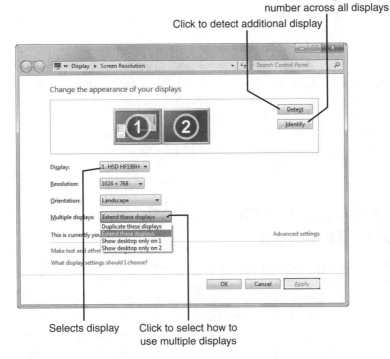

Click to flash large identifiying number across all displays

Click to detect additional display

Selects display   Click to select how to use multiple displays

FIGURE 2.14 Enabling a secondary display as an extended desktop.

▶ **Duplicate These Displays**—Makes your additional display
  mirror what's on the first display. You might need to adjust
  the resolution of the first display to match the second display to get this to work.

▶ **Extend These Displays**—Sets up an extended desktop. An
  extended desktop enables you to drag programs between
  windows and to maximize a program to its current window.

▶ **Show Desktop Only on (Specify Display Number)**—
  Disables the other display.

4. After making your selection, click **Apply**.

5. Click **Keep Changes** on the pop-up dialog that appears.

To make sure that both displays are set correctly, select the number to display and verify its resolution, as shown in the previous section. If you
want to use your display in the Portrait (long side vertical) mode or hang
the display upside down, use the **Orientation** menu to switch the setting
for each display. Click the **Advanced Settings** link if you need to make
any changes to color management, to the adapter properties, or to open up
a proprietary Control Panel made especially for your display. Click **OK** to
close the Screen Resolution dialog.

Adding Programs (Gadgets) to the Desktop

Windows 7 includes a number of small programs known as *gadgets*. You
can add these to your desktop by right-clicking an empty part of the desktop and selecting **Gadgets**. By default, Windows 7 includes nine different
gadgets (see Figure 2.15), but you can click the **Get More Gadgets
Online** to open up a web page where you can download more gadgets and
additional Windows 7 themes and desktop backgrounds. To download an
additional gadget, click the **Download** button for the gadget and follow the
directions for installing it.

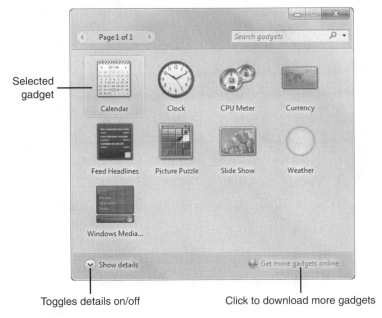

Selected
gadget

Toggles details on/off   Click to download more gadgets

FIGURE 2.15   Windows 7's desktop Gadgets menu.

To place a gadget on the desktop and adjust its settings:

1. Click it.

2. Drag it to desired location on the desktop.

To change the setting of a gadget, move your mouse to the right of the
gadget and click the Wrench (setup) icon to open the Options menu.
Figure 2.16 shows the Options menu for the Weather gadget.

To change the opacity of a gadget right-click it, select **Opacity**, and select
a percentage. You can also specify whether to keep the gadget always on
top of any other running programs.

FIGURE 2.16   Configuring options for the Weather gadget.

Summary

Windows 7 provides a number of ways to manage your desktop, including the ability to configure jump lists, change and create a theme, change your desktop background, add and configure a screen saver, select a sound scheme, change screen resolution, add and configure an additional display, and add and manage desktop gadgets. Use these options to make your desktop a reflection of your interests and work style.

LESSON 3

Working with Libraries

Windows 7's Libraries

When you open the Start menu and click Documents, Pictures, Music, or Videos, you open a new feature of Windows 7 known as *libraries*.

A library contains multiple folders, enabling you to see the contents of these folders at the same time. For example, the default contents of the Documents library include the current user's My Documents folder and the Public Documents folder. Likewise for music, pictures, and videos, each user's library contains the public folders and the user's individual folders for each content type. You can add any folder on a local or network hard disk to a library, so you can see the contents of external hard disks that contain pictures or other contents just by opening the appropriate library.

> NOTE: Folders on USB flash drives, CD or DVD drives, or other removable-media drives cannot be part of a library.

Windows 7's Backup and Restore function also uses libraries; any file stored in a local folder that's part of a library will be backed up.

> CAUTION: Files that are part of a library but are stored in network locations are not backed up by Windows 7's Backup and Restore function.

Seeing the Contents of a Library

To find out what folders a library includes:

1. Open the library.

2. Hover your mouse over the **Includes:** *x* **Locations** link (where x is a number).

As Figure 3.1 shows, this reveals the folders you can access through the library.

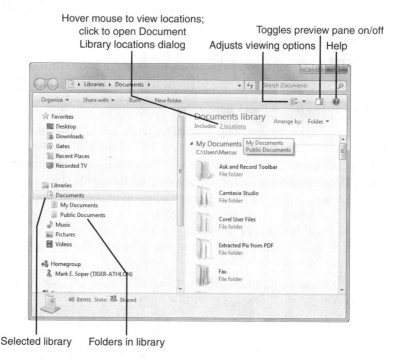

FIGURE 3.1 Viewing the locations in the Documents Library.

Use the icons above the library window to select a viewing style, to enable or disable the preview pane (see Figure 3.2), and to get help.

Adding a Folder to a Library

The normal contents of any library include the current user's folder and the public folder for that type of media. To add an additional folder to a library:

Click to turn off preview pane ─┐

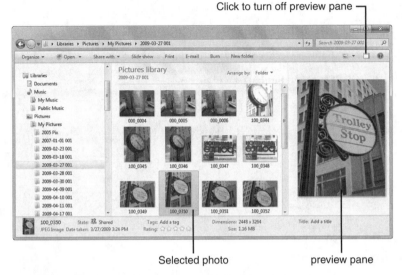

Selected photo   preview pane

FIGURE 3.2   The preview pane at work in the Pictures library.

1. Click the **Includes x Locations** link, as shown in Figure 3.1, to open the Library Locations dialog, such as the Documents Library Locations dialog shown in Figure 3.3.

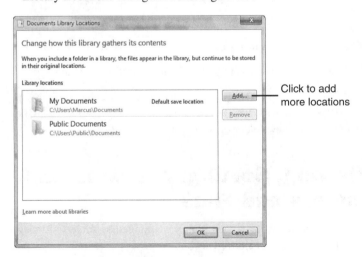

Click to add more locations

FIGURE 3.3   Use this dialog to add or remove folders from a library.

2. Click **Add** to add an additional location.

3. Navigate to the location you want to add to the library.

4. Highlight the folder you want to add.

5. Click **Include Folder** (see Figure 3.4).

1. Highlight folder

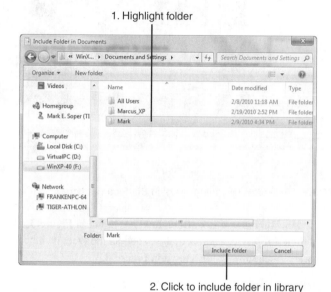

2. Click to include folder in library

FIGURE 3.4   Use this dialog to add or remove folders from a library.

The folder is now listed as part of a Library Location Is dialog.

Click **OK** to close the dialog. If you add a folder to a shared library, you are prompted to decide whether you want to share the new folder. Click **Yes** to share the new folder or **No** if you don't want to share it.

Viewing, Sorting, and Grouping Folders and Files

By default, the contents of each library is arranged by folders. To view the contents of a library in a different way:

1. Open the **Arrange By** menu.

2. Select a different option.

Each library offers a variety of Arrange By options appropriate for its contents.

Figure 3.5 is an example of the Date Modified view of the Documents library.

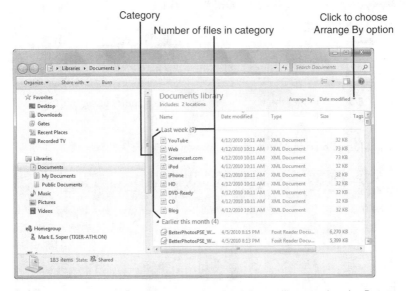

FIGURE 3.5   Viewing the contents of the Documents library using the Date Modified view.

Other Arrange By options for the Documents library include author, folder, tag, type, and name.

Figure 3.6 shows an example of the Arranged by Tag view of the Pictures library.

Other Arrange By options for the Pictures library include month, day, rating, and folder.

FIGURE 3.6 Viewing the contents of the Pictures library using the Tags view.

The Music library's Album view is shown in Figure 3.7.

FIGURE 3.7 Viewing the contents of the Music library using the Album view.

Other Arrange By options for the Music library include artist, song, genre, rating, and folder.

You can view videos by length, as in Figure 3.8.

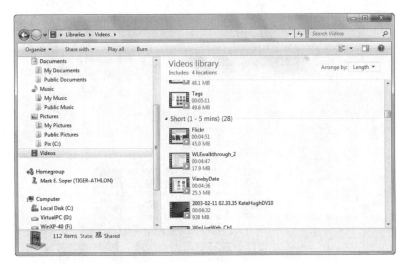

FIGURE 3.8   Viewing the contents of the Videos library using the Length view.

Other Arrange By options for the Videos library include year, type, name, and folder.

Choosing Additional Viewing Options

After selecting how you want to arrange the contents of a library, use the **More Options** menu to choose how to view the contents of that library:

1. Click **More Options**.

2. Select an option. Your choices include **Extra Large Icons**, **Large Icons**, **Medium Icons**, **Small Icons**, **List**, **Details**, **Tiles**, and **Content**.

3. The library pane display changes immediately.

The Extra Large Icons, Large Icons, and Medium Icons views are most suitable for use with the Pictures and Videos libraries because these views provide thumbnails of the contents. By using the slider control on computers running the Aero desktop, you can also continuously zoom the sizes of the icons so that you can select exactly the size you want, as shown in Figure 3.9.

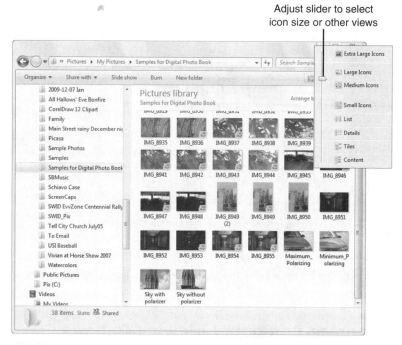

FIGURE 3.9   Using the slider to select a custom icon view size for the Pictures library.

The **Tiles** view shown in Figure 3.10 is useful with a variety of content types because it shows the name of the file, the type of file, the size of the file, and other information that varies with the file type.

FIGURE 3.10   Using the Tiles view in the Documents library to display a mix of file types.

The List view shown in Figure 3.11 and the similar Small Icons view (not shown) are helpful if you want to work with a large number of files at one time. With either view, it's easy to highlight the files that you want to copy, email, compress, copy, cut, or delete.

> TIP: To select a group of contiguous files, click the first file to select; then hold down Shift and click the last file. To select non-contiguous files, use Ctrl+Click instead of Shift+Click.

The Details view shown in Figure 3.12 provides a listing of the file or folder's date modified, type, and size and can be configured to show additional information.

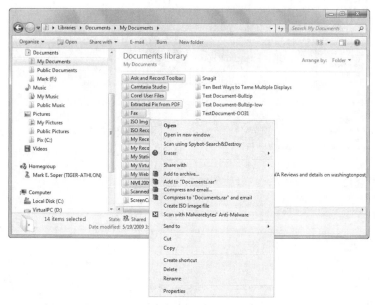

FIGURE 3.11   Selecting files in List view.

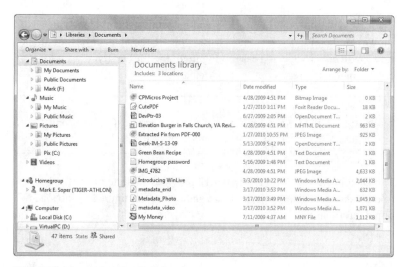

FIGURE 3.12   Using the Details view.

Sorting Files and Folders

You can sort files in any view, but it's easiest to sort files and to see the results of the sort when you use the Details view. By clicking at the top of each column, you can change the sort order.

1. To sort files by type (such as Microsoft Word, bitmap, MP3, AVI, and so on), click the **Type** column header (see Figure 3.13).

Click header to sort by header criteria

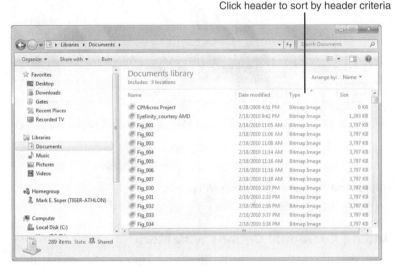

FIGURE 3.13   Sorting by type.

2. To sort by the date the file was last changed, click the **Date Modified** column header.

3. To change the sort order between ascending and descending, click the column header again.

By right-clicking an empty space within any library's file display, you can select **Sort By** and change what to sort by and whether to sort in ascending or descending order (see Figure 3.14). Click **More** to display an additional list of details that you can choose from.

Current sort type

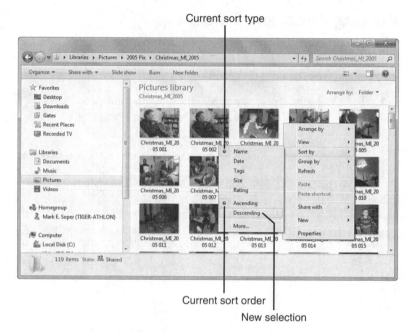

Current sort order
New selection

FIGURE 3.14   Viewing additional sort options.

Adding Additional Options with More

There are many additional columns you can add to each library's Details menu. To add columns

1. Select **More** from the right-click **Sort By** menu shown in Figure 3.14.

2. Currently selected columns are shown at the top of the list.

3. To add a column, scroll down the list and click the one you want (see Figure 3.15).

4. Repeat Step 3 until you have selected all of the columns you want.

> NOTE: Each library maintains its own list of columns in Details view.

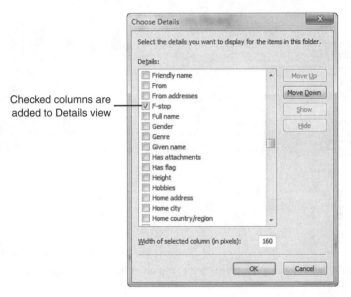

Checked columns are
added to Details view

FIGURE 3.15   Adding the F-Stop column to the Pictures library's Details
view.

Suggested Columns to Add

To make each library's Details view provide you with more of the information you need, consider adding the following columns for different libraries:

- ▶ **Documents**—Word Count (see Figure 3.16)

- ▶ **Pictures**—Camera Model (see Figure 3.17), White Balance, Exposure Program, ISO Speed, F- Stop, Type

- ▶ **Videos**—Data Rate, Length (see Figure 3.18)

- ▶ **Music**—Bit Rate, Genre (see Figure 3.19)

Word count

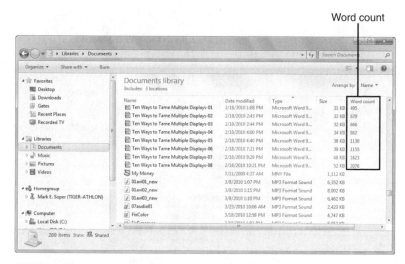

FIGURE 3.16 Using the Word Count column in the Documents library's Details view.

Camera model

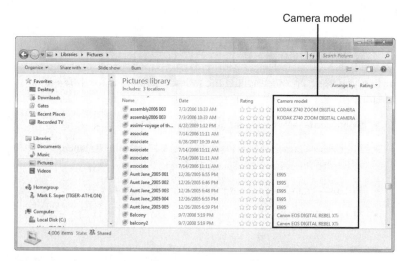

FIGURE 3.17 Using the Camera Model column in the Pictures library's Details view.

Length (hr:min:sec)

Date Rate

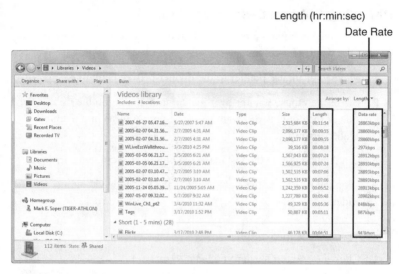

FIGURE 3.18   Using the Length and Data Rate columns in the Videos library's Details view.

Bit rate   Genre

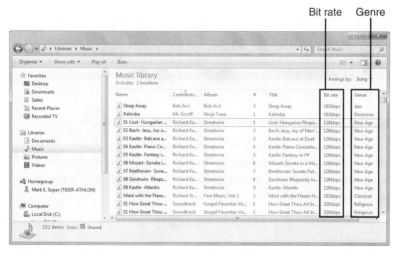

FIGURE 3.19   Using the Bit Rate and Genre columns in the Music library's Details view.

Changing Column Order and Width

You can change column widths and column order in Details view. To change the width of a column:

1. Move your mouse pointer to the divider between columns.

2. Hover the mouse pointer over the column divider on the right side of the column you want to adjust until it turns into a double-headed arrow.

3. Drag the pointer to the left make the highlighted column narrower.

4. Drag the pointer to the right to make the highlighted column wider.

To change column order:

1. Click the column header you want to move.

2. Drag it to the new position.

3. Release it.

To automatically fit columns to the available space, right-click a column header and select **Size Column to Fit** or select **Size All Columns to Fit** (see Figure 3.20). You can resize columns manually after using either of these operations. You can also select a column in the **Choose Details** dialog and adjust the width of the column (in pixels). Refer to Figure 3.15.

Removing and Adding Columns

To remove a column, right-click a column header and click any checked column name you want to remove. To add additional columns, scroll through the list and click any unchecked column. To see additional options, click **More**.

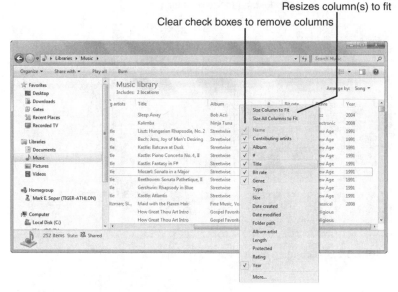

FIGURE 3.20   Adding and removing columns after right-clicking a column header.

Grouping Files and Folders

In addition to sorting files in the Pictures and Videos library by user-selectable criteria, you can also group files with the same criteria together in these libraries. To enable grouping:

1. Right-click an empty space in the current library view.

2. Select **Group By**.

3. Choose the criteria to use.

4. To select from the same additional criteria used for sorting, choose **More** from the **Group B**y menu.

5. To disable grouping, select **(None)** from the **Group By** criteria menu.

Figure 3.21 illustrates grouping pictures by F-stop (aperture).

F/stop (aperture) setting

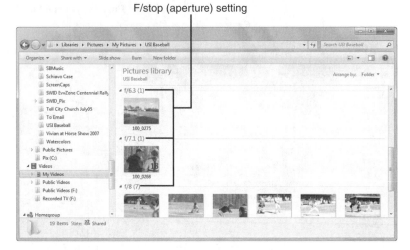

FIGURE 3.21   Grouping pictures by F-stop (aperture).

Learning More About a File

When you select a file in a library or any other location, Windows 7 displays file properties at the bottom of the Windows Explorer dialog. By default, Windows 7 uses the medium-size properties window illustrated in Figure 3.22.

To adjust the amount of information in the properties window:

1. Right-click the properties window.

2. Select the size desired.

3. To see less information, select **Small** (see Figure 3.23).

4. To see more information, select **Large** (see Figure 3.24)

> NOTE: By comparing Figures 3.22–3.24, you can see that the more file properties information that's visible, the less room you have in the library window to view files.

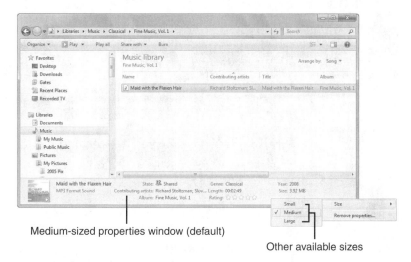

Medium-sized properties window (default)

Other available sizes

FIGURE 3.22 The default medium-size properties view for a file in the Music library.

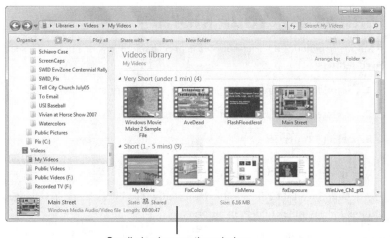

Small-sized properties window

FIGURE 3.23 The small-sized properties view for a file in the Videos library.

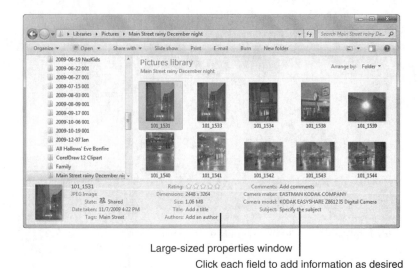

Large-sized properties window
Click each field to add information as desired

FIGURE 3.24   The large-size properties view for a file in the Pictures library.

Managing Your Library

Windows 7 includes a variety of options for managing your library. To see these settings:

1. Scroll to the Libraries portion of the left pane of any library view.

2. Right-click the library you want to manage.

3. Select **Properties**.

A typical library properties menu is shown in Figure 3.25.

The default Save folder location is indicated with a check mark. To change settings for any other folders in a library:

1. Right-click the folder.

2. Select **Set as Default Save Location** to make it the new default.

3. Click **Remove** to remove the folder from the list.

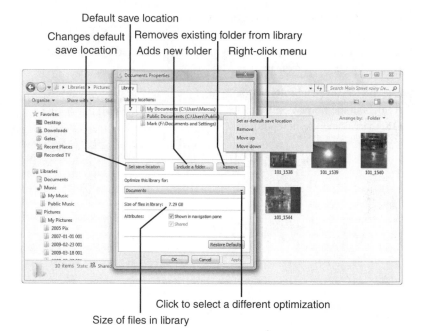

FIGURE 3.25   Managing the Documents library.

4. Click **Move Up** to move the folder higher in the list.

5. Click **Move Down** to move the folder lower in the list.

To add a folder to a library:

1. Click **Include a Folder**.

2. Navigate to the folder location.

3. Select the folder.

4. Click **Include Folder**.

To change the default appearance of a library, select the appropriate option from the **Optimize This Library For** menu. The total size of the files and folder in the library is shown beneath the Optimize pull-down menu.

Use the **Attributes** check boxes to determine whether the library will be shared and whether it will appear in the Navigation pane. If the library is shared as part of a homegroup, you must change the homegroup setting if you no longer want to share it.

Use the **Restore Defaults** button to reset the library to its original settings (folders in the library, optimization, and so on). Click **Apply**; then click **OK** to save and use new settings.

LESSON 4

Enjoying Photos and Media

Windows 7 Media Tools

Windows 7 Home Premium, Professional, and Ultimate editions feature several media playback programs, including Windows Photo Viewer, Windows Media Player, and Windows Media Center. Windows Photo Viewer provides convenient windowed or full-screen viewing of your digital photos, whereas Windows Media Player and Windows Media Center also support music and video playback. Windows 7 also includes a wizard to help you print your photos in a variety of sizes.

Starting Windows Photo Viewer

Windows Photo Viewer provides windowed or full-screen playback for common digital photo file types such as JPEG and TIFF and can also be used to view RAW files after you install the appropriate RAW codec. Here's how to open a photo with Windows Photo Viewer:

1. Click **Start**.

2. Click **Pictures**.

3. Navigate to the picture you want to view.

4. Choose from one of the following:

> ▶ If you have not installed any other photo-viewing or photo-editing programs, double-click the photo or right-click it and select **Preview** (see Figure 4.1).

> ▶ If you have installed other photo-viewing or photo-editing programs, right-click the photo, select **Open With**, and select **Photo Viewer** from the list of programs (see Figure 4.2).

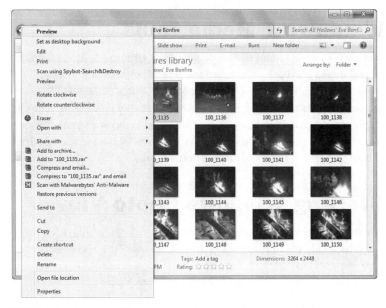

FIGURE 4.1   Opening Windows Photo Viewer with Preview.

FIGURE 4.2   Opening Windows Photo Viewer from the Open With menu.

Using Windows Photo Viewer

The Windows Photo Viewer display is shown in Figure 4.3.

Use the controls along the bottom of the screen (from left to right) to:

► Adjust picture magnification

► Toggle between full-image view and actual size view

► Move to previous photo

► Start slide show

► Move to next photo

► Rotate photo to left (counterclockwise)

► Rotate photo to right (clockwise)

► Delete photo

FIGURE 4.3   Windows Photo Viewer.

Adjusting Picture Magnification

Windows Photo Viewer automatically scales photos to fit in the current window. If you want to see how sharp your photo is, or need to view a portion of your photo, adjusting the magnification is helpful. Here's how:

1. Open the photo in Windows Photo Viewer.

2. Click the slider at the left end of the controls below the photo and move it upward until you reach the desired magnification (see Figure 4.4).

To adjust what portion of the picture fits into the display window:

1. Move the mouse pointer into the photo. The default pointer turns into a hand.

2. Click and drag the photo until you see the desired portion of the photo inside the Windows Photo Viewer window.

3. Release the mouse button.

FIGURE 4.4   Adjusting magnification in Windows Photo Viewer.

NOTE: The magnification adjustments affect only viewing size; print size is set by the settings used by your printer.

Rotating Photos

If you like to shoot vertical photos, it can be irritating to view them until they're rotated to the correct orientation. To rotate a photo:

1. Open the photo in Windows Photo Viewer.

2. If the top of the photo faces left, click the right curved arrow. If the top of the photo faces right, click the left curved arrow.

3. Click the forward or back arrows to save changes to the current photo and display another photo.

Figure 4.5 compares a vertical photo before and after rotation.

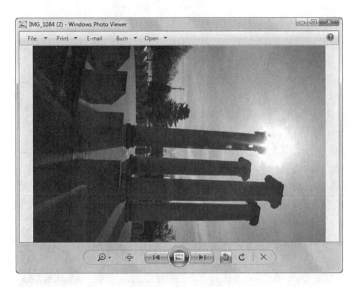

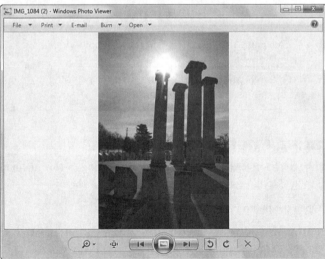

FIGURE 4.5   Rotating a photo with Windows Photo Viewer.

NOTE: You cannot rotate a photo stored on read-only media, such as a recordable CD or DVD. If you need to rotate a photo stored on read-only media, copy it to your hard disk and then rotate it.

Viewing Your Photos in a Slide Show

To view the photos in the current folder as a slide show, click the **Slide Show** button, as shown in Figure 4.3. Each photo displays full-screen.

By default, slide shows play in a loop at medium speed. However, you can also advance to the next or previous photo manually, pause the show, shuffle picture order, and select fast or slow playback speeds. To adjust playback options, do the following:

1. Right-click the display after starting the slide show.

2. Select the option(s) wanted (see Figure 4.6).

FIGURE 4.6   Slide show playback options in Windows Photo Viewer.

3. Click away from the menu to put changes into effect.

4. To close the show and return to the normal Windows Photo Viewer display, click **Exit**.

Using the File Menu

The File menu includes options to:

▶ Delete the current photo.

▶ Make a copy of the current photo into any folder.

▶ Copy the photo to the Windows Clipboard.

▶ Display image properties, including exposure metadata (see Figure 4.7).

FIGURE 4.7   Viewing exposure metadata.

▶ Exit the program.

Using the Print Menu

The Print menu provides two ways to print:

▶ Select **Print** to make prints with your own printer.

▶ Select **Order Prints** to order photos from a variety of online photo print providers (see Figure 4.8).

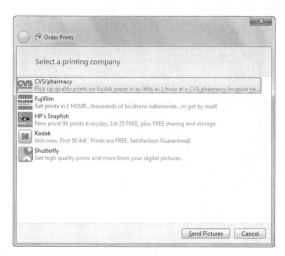

FIGURE 4.8   Preparing to order prints from an online provider.

> TIP: If you want to order prints from multiple photos, I recommend installing Windows Live Photo Gallery. You can select multiple prints and use its Print menu to order prints. Learn more at http://download.live.com.

To learn more about printing photos with any Windows 7 application, see "Printing a Picture" later in this lesson.

Emailing a Picture

Windows 7 does not include an email program. However, after you install an email program such as Windows Live Mail (available as part of Windows Live Essentials) or others, you can use the E-Mail menu to email photos. Using Windows Photo Viewer to email your photos enables you to send a reduced-size version of your photo that's easier for recipients to view and takes less time to download and upload. Here's how to do it:

1. Select a photo you want to email.

2. Click **E-Mail**.

3. Select the size of photo you want to email (see Figure 4.9).

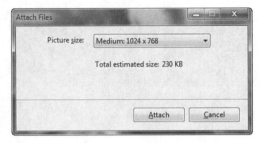

FIGURE 4.9   Creating a smaller-sized version of a photo to email.

4. Click **Attach**.

NOTE: The default photo dimensions are 1024×768 (medium).
Other sizes include 640×480 (smallest); 800×600 (small);
1280×1024 (large); and original size.

5. Your email program opens, creates a message, and attaches the
photo to the message (see Figure 4.10).

FIGURE 4.10   Windows Photo Viewer attaches your photo to an email
message.

6. Enter the recipient's address.

7. Add other text as desired.

8. Send the message.

> NOTE: If you use Windows Live Mail, you might be asked if you want to create a photo email. A photo email stores a photo online using Windows Live Skydrive, embeds a small thumbnail in the message, and includes a link to the photo.
>
> By creating a photo email, you can send a photo in its original size without filling up the recipient's email inbox.

Printing a Picture

Windows 7 automatically uses its Print Pictures Wizard whenever you select Print from within Windows Photo Viewer or after selecting one or more photos from Windows Explorer.

The Print Pictures Wizard (see Figure 4.11) provides options for:

- ▶ Selecting the printer
- ▶ Paper size
- ▶ Print quality
- ▶ Paper type
- ▶ Print layout
- ▶ Number of copies of each picture
- ▶ Whether to fit pictures to frame
- ▶ Printer options

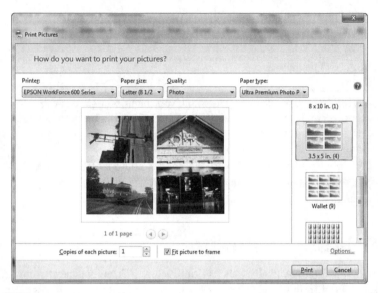

FIGURE 4.11   Using Print Pictures to print four pictures on a single sheet of paper.

> TIP: Physical printers connected to your computer, physical printers shared over a network, and virtual printers that create PDF, XPS, or other files are all listed in the Printer menu. Print Pictures "remembers" the last printer selection made.
>
> Network printers are listed as *computername**printername*.

To print your photos, do this:

1. Select the picture or pictures you want to print.

2. Click **Print**. The Print Picture Wizard opens.

3. Select the printer you want to use.

4. Select the paper size.

5. Choose the print quality.

6. Choose the paper type.

7. Select the number of copies of each picture to print.

8. Select the layout.

9. Click **Print**.

Photo-Printing Tips and Tricks

Paper size, quality, and paper type settings vary with the printer you select. To see additional paper sizes, click **More**.

By default, Print Pictures lists only photo papers in its **Paper Type** menu. To see other options, such as **Plain Paper**, follow these steps:

1. Click the **Options** link (see Figure 4.11) to open the Print Settings dialog.

2. Click **Printer Properties.**

3. Select the paper type.

4. Click **OK** to close the dialog.

By default, Print Pictures lists only photo-optimized quality settings in its **Quality** menu. To see other options:

1. Follow the previous set of instructions to select the paper type.

2. Open the **Quality** menu.

3. Select the desired option.

> CAUTION: Make sure you select a paper type that matches the paper you use, or your photo prints might be of poor quality.

The Print Settings dialog includes links to help you get better prints. Use the **Color Management** link to select the correct printer profile for your printer. Use the **Printer Properties** link to view and select additional paper types, check ink levels, and perform additional printer-specific tasks.

Using Windows Media Player

Although Windows Media Player can play video, DVD movies, and photos, its most common use is for music and audio file playback. The following sections show you how to perform common tasks with music files. These methods can also be used to work with other types of files.

To start Windows Media Player:

1. Click **Start**.

2. Hover the mouse over **All Programs**.

3. Scroll down to Windows Media Player.

4. Click **Windows Media Player**.

5. The first time you start Windows Media Player, you are prompted to select **Recommended** or **Custom Settings**. If you want to use recommended settings, click **Finish**. To use custom settings, click **Custom Settings**, click **Next**, and provide the information requested.

6. Windows Media Player opens to the Album view of the Music library (see Figure 4.12).

FIGURE 4.12   Windows Media Player playing an audio CD.

NOTE: To turn on the menu bar shown in Figure 4.12, click **Organize**, **Layout**, **Show Menu Bar**.

Playing and Ripping an Audio CD

Windows Media Player can convert audio CDs into digital music files (a process called "ripping") or play the music on the CD. To play an audio CD:

1. Insert the CD into the optical drive on the computer.

2. Windows Media Player reads the CD tracks.

3. The CD starts playing automatically (see Figure 4.13).

FIGURE 4.13   Windows Media Player playing an audio CD.

CDs can be ripped into your choice of several different digital formats. The most popular are Windows Media Audio (WMA) and MP3. To select a format and a bit rate:

1. Click **Tools**.

2. Click **Options**.

3. Click the **Rip Music** tab (see Figure 4.14).

FIGURE 4.14   Windows Media Player's Rip Music tab configured for automatic ripping and ejection of CDs and the highest bit rate for creating MP3 audio files.

4. Open the **Format** menu and select the format desired.

5. Adjust the **Audio Quality** slider to select the bit rate desired.

6. To rip CDs automatically, click the **Rip CD Automatically** check box. This setting takes effect after you insert a new CD.

7. To automatically eject the CD after ripping, click the **Eject CD After Ripping** check box.

8. Click **Apply**.

9. Click **OK**.

> TIP: Unless you have a portable media player that can play only WMA files, I recommend creating MP3 files. The default sampling rates for WMA and MP3 files are suitable for creating music for portable media players. However, if you are building a digital media library for playback on high-quality speakers, consider increasing the bit rate. This can result in higher-quality audio but also larger file sizes.

To rip the CD manually:

1. Right-click the CD icon in the left pane.

2. Select **Rip CD** to Library.

3. A progress bar appears next to each track in the middle pane.

4. At the end of the process, the CD is listed in the Album/Music library.

5. You can eject the CD manually if you did not select the option to automatically eject the CD.

Creating a Playlist

A playlist is a list of songs you can play, burn to CD, or sync to a portable media device. To create and save a playlist, do the following:

1. Select a song, video, or photo.

2. Drag it to the **Playlist** pane on the right side of the Windows Media Player interface.

3. Repeat Steps 1 and 2 until your playlist is complete.

4. Click **Save List**.

5. Enter a name for the list in the **Name** field above the list of songs (see Figure 4.15).

FIGURE 4.15   Creating a playlist.

Syncing Files to a Portable Media Device

When you sync files to a portable media device, you can sync a saved playlist or create a new list. To sync files from a playlist, do the following:

1. Connect the portable media device to your computer.

2. Windows Media Player switches to the **Sync** tab.

3. Click **Playlists** in the right pane.

4. Drag a playlist to the **Sync** pane.

5. Repeat Step 4 until you have added all the playlists you want to the sync list.

6. Click **Start Sync** (see Figure 4.16).

7. Disconnect the device when you see the Sync Completed message.

8. Click the **Click Here** link to display the results of the file synchronization.

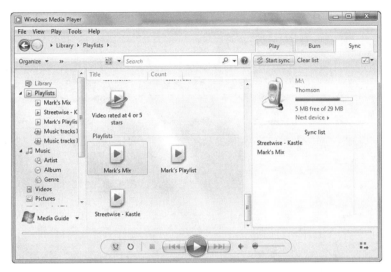

FIGURE 4.16 Synchronizing a playlist to a portable media player.

NOTE: To sync individual media files instead of a playlist, select individual media files and drag them to the sync list in Steps 3–5.

Burning an Audio CD

Windows Media Player makes it easy to create an audio mix CD of your musical favorites. Here's how to create an audio CD:

1. Click the **Burn** tab.

2. Insert a blank CD.

3. Drag playlists or individual songs to the burn list.

4. To change the order of a music track, drag it to the preferred location.

5. Click **Start Burn** (see Figure 4.17).

FIGURE 4.17   Preparing to burn an audio CD.

6. At the end of the burn process, the CD is ejected.

> TIP: Use CD-R media if you want to create a disc that can be played on the widest range of CD players. If you have players that can use CD-RW media, you can use CD-RW discs to create an audio mix CD for short-term use. You can erase the contents of a CD-RW disc using Windows Explorer.

To create a playlist from the burn list:

1. Click the first file in the burn list.

2. Press and hold either Shift key.

3. Click the last file in the burn list. All files should now be highlighted.

4. Right-click the highlighted burn list.

5. Select **Add To** and then **Additional Playlists**.

6. Click **Create Playlist**.

7. Enter a name in place of **New Playlist** (see Figure 4.18).

8. Click **OK**.

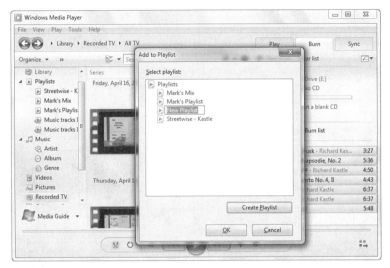

FIGURE 4.18   Creating a playlist from a burn list.

Using Windows Media Center

Windows Media Center, like Windows Media Player, can play all types of media supported by Windows. However, Windows Media Center can also watch and record TV on computers equipped with a TV tuner. Because it can be used to watch and record TV, Windows Media Center is designed primarily for use with big-screen TVs and home theater systems. It includes a 10-foot UI (user interface) and support for optional infrared (IR) remote controls.

Initial Setup

Windows Media Center must be configured before you can use it. Here's how to perform initial setup.

1. Click **Start**.

2. Hover the mouse over **All Programs**.

3. Click **Windows Media Center**.

4. When the Windows Media Center window opens, click **Continue**.

5. The Get Started dialog appears. Click **Express** to perform basic setup.

6. Windows Media Center displays its main menu (see Figure 4.19). Each major category, such as Movies, Music, and so on, is often called a "stripe."

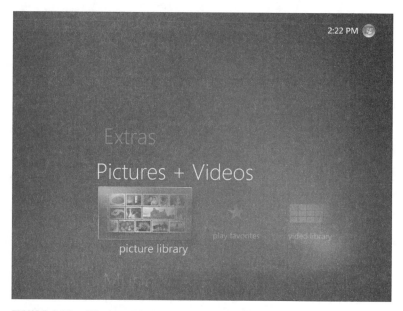

FIGURE 4.19   Windows Media Center's main menu.

NOTE: If you have a TV tuner, you also need to connect it to your TV source (broadcast, cable, and so on) and configure it before you can watch TV with Windows Media Center. To configure your TV tuner, click **Tasks**, **Settings**, **TV**, **TV Signal**, **Set Up TV Signal**, and follow the prompts. To learn more, see the online articles "Setting Up and Watching ATSC with Windows Media Center"at http://www. informit.com/articles/article.aspx?p=1396502 and "Windows 7 Feature Focus: Windows Media Center" at http://www.maximumpc. com/article/news/windows_7_feature_focus_windows_media_ center.

Navigating Through Windows Media Center

You can use a mouse and keyboard or a Windows Media Center-compatible remote control with Windows Media Center. Use the following methods to navigate Windows Media Center with a mouse and keyboard:

▶ To return to the main menu, click the green Windows Media Center icon at the upper-left corner of the current dialog.

▶ To return to the previous dialog, click the left arrow next to the Windows Media Center icon in the upper-left corner.

▶ To scroll horizontally, move the mouse to the left or right edge of the screen and click the arrow that appears.

▶ To scroll vertically, use the mouse's scroll wheel.

▶ To move in any direction (up/down/left/right) with the keyboard, use the directional arrows.

▶ To control playback of videos or music, use the DVD/VCR-style control cluster in the lower-right corner.

Figure 4.20 illustrates the on-screen controls just listed.

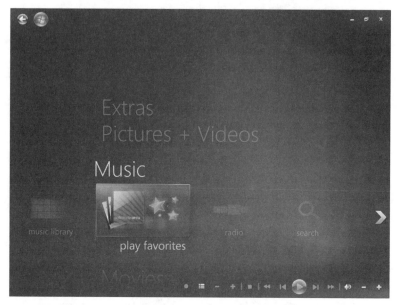

FIGURE 4.20   Windows Media Center mouse-based navigation controls.

Setting Up Libraries

By default, Windows Media Center displays media found in the current user's Pictures, Music, and Videos libraries and recorded TV and movies folders on the current system. To add additional locations on the same computer or other computers on the network, follow these steps:

1. Click the green Windows Media Center icon in the upper left-hand corner (if you are using a mouse), or press the Windows Media Center **Home** button on your Windows Media Center remote control.

2. Click **Tasks**.

3. Click **Settings**.

4. Click **Media Libraries**.

5. Select the media library to manage; in this example, we work with the recorded TV library (see Figure 4.21).

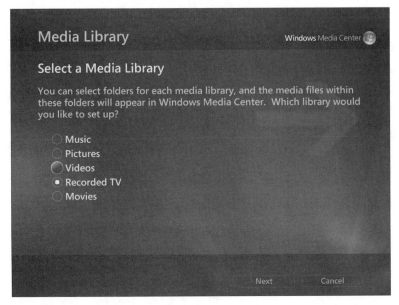

FIGURE 4.21   Selecting a media library.

6. Click **Next**.

7. Select whether to add or remove folders from the library.

8. Click **Next**.

9. Select where to browse for folders: This Computer; Another Computer; Manually Add a Folder (in this example, we choose **Another Computer**).

10. Click **Next**.

11. Scroll down to the location you want to add.

12. Click the empty check box for the location (see Figure 4.22); you can scroll and select multiple locations in this step.

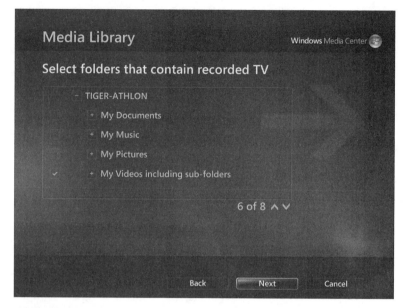

FIGURE 4.22   Adding the My Videos folder from a network computer to a Windows Media Center library.

13. Click **Next**.

14. To complete the process, click **Finish**.

NOTE: To add or remove other locations (folders), click **No** in Step 14 and continue as prompted.

Playing Media with Windows Media Center

The following sections discuss how to play back videos and photos from Windows Media Center. The methods in these examples are similar to those used to play back other types of media, such as recorded TV shows, music, and movies.

All TV shows, including Internet TV, live TV, recorded TV and movies recorded from broadcast, cable, and so on, are accessed from the TV menu stripe. Movies on DVD, Blu-ray (when you add a third-party Blu-ray player), or ripped from those media, are accessed from the Movie menu stripe. All music tracks on CD, ripped from CD, or downloaded from the Internet, are accessed from the Music menu stripe.

Video Playback

Videos other than those recorded from TV are viewed in the Video Library section. To view videos from the main menu:

1. Click **Pictures + Videos**.

2. Click **Video Library.**

3. Click the wanted view: Folders, Date Taken, or Shared.

4. Highlight an item to see details (see Figure 4.23).

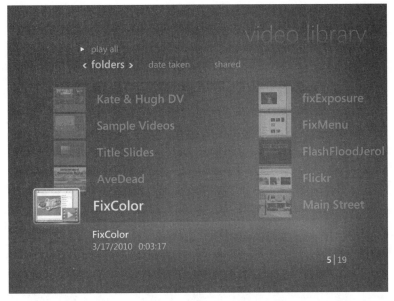

FIGURE 4.23   Selecting a video in the Video Library's default Folders view.

5. Navigate to the video you want to play, and click it.

6. To play all videos in the current view, click **Play All**.

NOTE: The Shared view in any Windows Media Center library lists media residing on another computer on the network. When you play back shared media, you might see a *Buffering x%* message appear before and during playback, and pauses during playback.

Viewing Photos

Digital pictures and scanned photos are viewed in the Picture Library section of the Pictures + Videos task. To view pictures from the main menu:

1. Click **Pictures + Videos**.

2. Click **Picture Library**.

3. Click the wanted view: Folders, Tags, Date Taken, Ratings, Slide Shows, or Shared. Figure 4.24 illustrates a typical Date Taken view.

FIGURE 4.24   Viewing Picture Library by Date Taken.

4. Click to navigate to the specific item you want to view.

5. Click a photo to view it individually.

6. To view all photos in the current view, click **Play Slide Show**.

7. To stop playback, press the Esc key or click the square **Stop** button in the media playback control cluster (see Figure 4.20).

LESSON 5

Managing Devices and Printers

Accessing Devices and Printers

The Devices and Printers applet is a new feature of Windows 7. It provides complete access to the devices and printers installed in your machine and computer. To access Devices and Printers:

1. Open the **Start** menu.

2. Click **Devices and Printers**.

3. If Devices and Printers are not listed on the Start menu, click **Control Panel**.

4. From Control Panel, click **Hardware and Sound.**

5. From the Devices and Printers category, click **Devices and Printers** (see Figure 5.1).

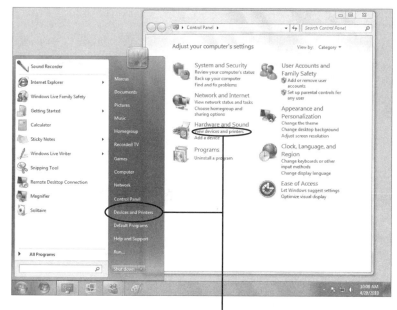

Click to open Devices and Printers

FIGURE 5.1   Accessing Devices and Printers from the Start menu or Control Panel.

Navigating Devices and Printers

Devices and Printers (see Figure 5.2) includes two categories: At the top of the dialog are the devices associated with your computer, such as the computer itself and its internal drives, displays, mouse and keyboard, scanners, external storage, and others.

The second part of the dialog includes printers, faxes, and multifunction devices. These devices can connect directly to your computer, made available through the network, or are software-based virtual output devices such as the Microsoft XPS Document Writer or programs that create PDF files.

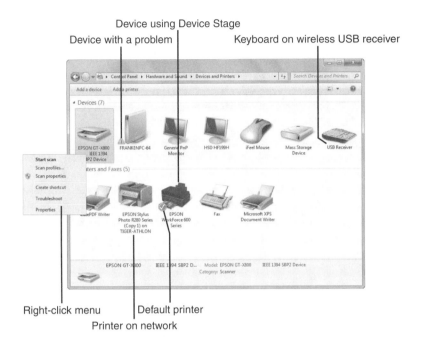

FIGURE 5.2   A typical Devices and Printers dialog.

Managing Devices

To begin managing a device, right-click the device to see the options available for that device (see Figure 5.2). By using Devices and Printers and the
right-click menu, you can access parts of the Windows 7 interface that
would've required moving through many different menus in previous editions of Windows. The following sections provide you with a quick guide
to managing the most common devices that you'll find in the Devices and
Printers dialog.

Computer

Your computer is listed by its computer name in Devices and Printers. The
following sections describe the options you can choose from the right-
click menu.

Browse Files

This option displays files and folders on any drive installed on the computer, including the system hard disk, other hard disks, CD or DVD drives, and floppy drives (see Figure 5.3). Choose a drive to open it in Windows Explorer.

You can also select **Browse Files** from the top-level menu.

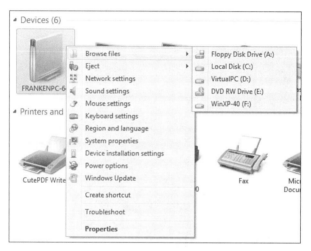

FIGURE 5.3 Preparing to browse drives.

NOTE: If you try to browse a removable-media (CD, DVD, flash memory, or floppy) drive that has no media, the system will pause for a few moments and might display an error message.

Eject

This option ejects media from the onboard CD or DVD drive. If you need to close the media before it is ejected, you will be prompted for the appropriate option. You can also choose **Eject** from the menu above the **Devices** list.

Network Settings

This option opens the Network and Sharing Center. Learn more about using the Network and Sharing Center in Lesson 9, "Connecting to Other Windows Computers."

Sound Settings

This option opens the Sound properties sheet so that you can adjust playback, recording, system sounds (see Figure 5.4), or communications settings.

FIGURE 5.4   The Sound properties sheet's Sounds tab.

Mouse Settings

This option opens the Mouse properties sheet, enabling you to control button configuration, pointers, pointer options (see Figure 5.5), mouse wheel, and view hardware properties.

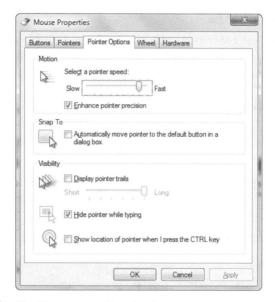

FIGURE 5.5   The Mouse properties sheet.

Keyboard Settings

This option opens the Keyboard properties sheet, providing options for character repeat, cursor blink rate, and keyboard properties.

Region and Language

These options enable you to change keyboard or input language, install or uninstall language packs (Windows 7 Ultimate edition only), select different date/time and numeric formats for data, and perform various administrative tasks.

System Properties

This option displays the System properties sheet (see Figure 5.6) with access to Device Manager, remote settings, system protection, and advanced system settings.

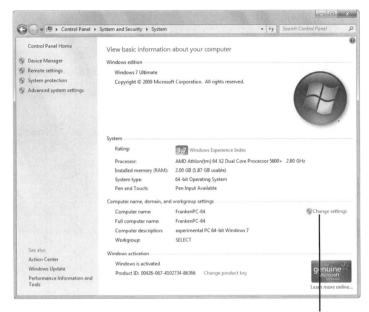

Click to change computer or
workgroup name or join domain

FIGURE 5.6   The System properties sheet.

CAUTION: Changing advanced system settings such as performance, startup and recovery, and environmental variables are best done under expert supervision. You could slow down your computer or cause it to malfunction if you don't know what you're doing.

Device Installation Settings

This option enables you to configure whether to download driver software and realistic icons for devices. By default this is enabled.

Power Options

This opens the Power Options dialog (see Figure 5.7) enabling you to select from different power plans, create a power plan, and configure when to turn off the display, when the computer should sleep, whether to require a password on wakeup, or configure power buttons.

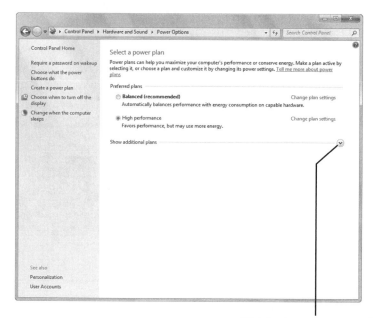

Click to show other power plans

FIGURE 5.7   The Power Options dialog.

Windows Update

This option opens the Windows Update dialog (see Figure 5.8) so that you can install updates, view update history, check for updates, and configure Windows Update.

Click to choose additional updates   Click to install updates

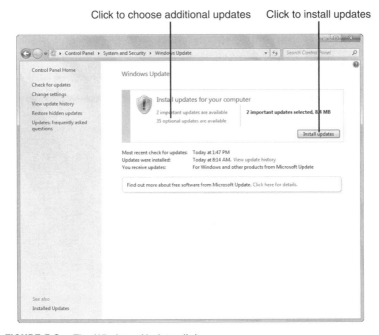

FIGURE 5.8   The Windows Update dialog.

Display (Monitor, Projector, HDTV)

Right-click each display listed and select **Display Settings** to open the
Screen Resolution dialog (see Figure 5.9). Use this dialog to adjust screen
resolution, set up multiple displays, and make advanced settings.

To add an additional display and extend the desktop to the additional display do the following:

1. Make sure the display is plugged into the computer and turned on.

2. Open **Devices and Printers**.

3. Right-click the display and select **Display Settings**.

4. Click **Detect** and the icon for the additional display appears.

5. Open the **Multiple Displays** menu.

6. Select **Extend These Displays**.

7. Click **Apply**, then **OK**.

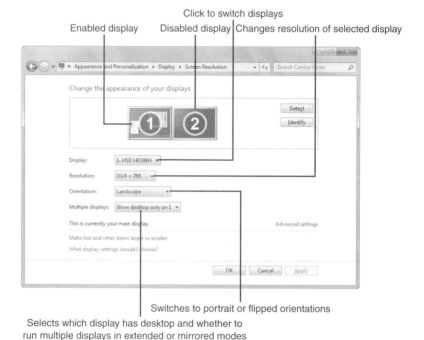

FIGURE 5.9   The Display Settings dialog.

You can then drag program windows from the primary display to the additional display.

Mass Storage Device

The Mass Storage Device category is used for external USB and FireWire drives and for flash memory card readers. When media is connected or

inserted, right-clicking the **Mass Storage Device** icon displays the
AutoPlay, Browse Files, and Eject options (see Figure 5.10). Click the triangle next to each of these options to choose the drive.

Click to choose drive to use

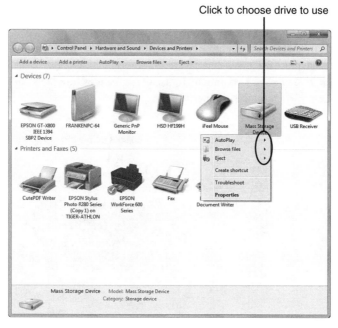

FIGURE 5.10   Options for mass storage device.

You can also select **AutoPlay**, **Browse Files**, or **Eject** from the top-level
menu.

CAUTION: Before you disconnect a USB hard disk or removable-
media drive, use Eject to make sure read and write operations are
finished. Disconnect the drive when you see the message that it's
safe to remove it.

Scanner

Scanners (and multifunction devices featuring scanning capabilities) include the following options on the right-click menu.

Start Scan

This selection launches the scanning software built into Windows 7 (see Figure 5.11). However, keep in mind that Windows 7 does not support advanced features that might be built into your scanner, such as transparency adapters for slides and negatives, dust reduction features such as DigitalICE, and color restoration. To use these features, use the scanning software provided by the scanner vendor.

FIGURE 5.11   Windows 7's scanning software.

Scan Profiles

This option enables you to select and create settings to use for scanning different types of photos and to specify a scan profile to use by default (see Figure 5.12). The default scan profile is used when **Start Scan** is run.

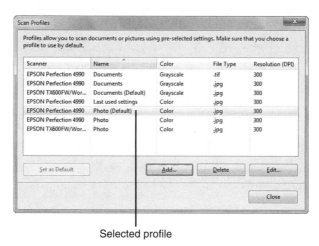

Selected profile

FIGURE 5.12   Scan profiles on a system with a scanner and an all-in-one unit.

Scan Properties

Use the **Test Scanner** button on the **General** tab to verify proper scanner operation. Use the **Advanced** tab to determine what happens when you press a button on the scanner. Use the **Color Management** tab to set up color management settings for the scanner. Figure 5.13 illustrates these options.

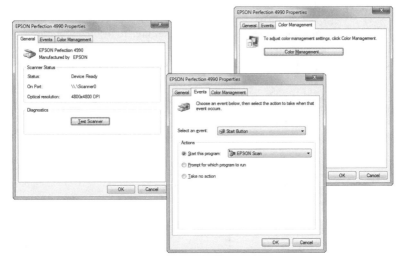

FIGURE 5.13 Options on the Scan Properties sheet.

Managing Printers and Faxes

Windows 7 groups printers, faxes, and multifunction devices into the Printers and Faxes category of Devices and Printers. You can manage print jobs, device functions, and other settings for these devices.

Common Options

All devices in the Printers and Faxes group include the following settings on the right-click menu:

- ▶ **See What's Printing**—Displays the print queue for the current device (see Figure 5.14).

- ▶ **Set as Default Printer**—Selects the current printer as the default printer.

- ▶ **Printing Preferences**—Opens the preferences dialog for the current printer or device. Use **Printing Preferences** (Figure 5.15 shows a typical example) to configure paper type, print quality, and other print options, and to perform maintenance functions such as checking ink levels or cleaning printheads.

▶ **Printer Properties**—Opens the property sheet for the current printer or device. Use **Printer Properties** to print a test page (**General** tab), set up sharing (**Sharing** tab), configure availability and advanced spooler settings (**Advanced** tab), configure color management (**Color Management** tab), set security options (**Security** tab), and view driver version (**Version Information** tab).

FIGURE 5.14   Viewing a print queue.

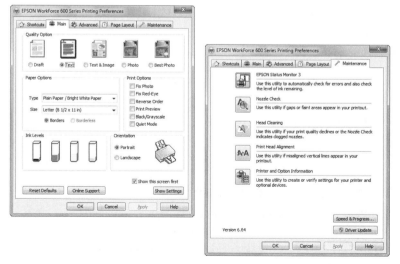

FIGURE 5.15   The Main and Maintenance tabs from a typical all-in-one unit's Printing preferences dialog.

Multifunction Device

Multifunction devices are designed to perform printing and scanning functions, and some devices also include fax functions. For this reason, the right-click menu for a multifunction device includes support for printing, scanning, and any other options available on the device. If the devices have provision for one or more flash memory cards, the **Browse Files** option is also available (see Figure 5.16).

FIGURE 5.16   The right-click menu for a multifunction device with flash memory card slots.

Print Server Properties

The **Print Server Properties** menu option appears only when you select a printer, although it deals with settings for all installed printers. The **Printer Server Properties** sheet includes the following tabs:

▶ **Forms**—Configures different sizes of forms for your printers

▶ **Ports**—Displays ports in use on your print server

▶ **Drivers**—Lists available printer drivers, and provides options for adding and removing printer drivers and viewing printer driver properties

▶ **Security**—Configures who can use the printer and who can configure special features of the installed printers

▶ **Advanced**—Displays the location of the print spooler folder used for storing print jobs and configures whether to show informational notifications for local or network printers

Managing Multifunction Devices More Easily with Device Stage

Multifunction devices with realistic icons use a new type of driver known as **Device Stage**. Double-click the device icon in Devices and Printers to access all device features, including manufacturer information about the device; full access to printer and scanner features, including the manufacturer's own scan utility; and product support, including paper and media ordering. Figure 5.17 illustrates the Device Stage dialog for the Epson WorkForce 600 series.

> TIP: If you don't have a realistic icon for your multifunction device in Devices and Printers, it's not using a Device Stage driver. Your device will work with a standard driver, but if you install an updated driver, you might get a Device Stage-compatible driver. Check your vendor's website for an updated driver.

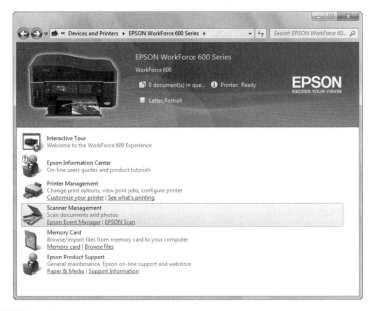

FIGURE 5.17   A Device Stage driver interface.

Installing or Removing a Device or Printer

In most cases, Windows 7 automatically detects new devices and installs them for you. However, you can also start the installation process by clicking **Add a Device** or **Add a Printer** from the top-level menu.

1. When you select **Add a Device**, Windows searches for devices and any new devices that are discovered are listed.

2. When you select **Add a Printer**, Windows opens the **Add Printer Wizard**.

3. Choose the appropriate option and click **Next** to continue.

4. Click **Remove Device** to remove the currently selected device.

5. To confirm your choice, click **Yes**; to cancel the removal process, click **No**.

Troubleshooting a Device

Devices or printers with problems display an ! sign next to their icons in Devices and Printers. To troubleshoot the device, follow these steps:

1. Right-click the device and select **Troubleshoot** (see Figure 5.18). The troubleshooter scans the selected device for problems and displays a brief report.

FIGURE 5.18   Preparing to troubleshoot a problem with a computer.

2. Click **View Details** to open the properties sheet for the device for more information (see Figure 5.19).

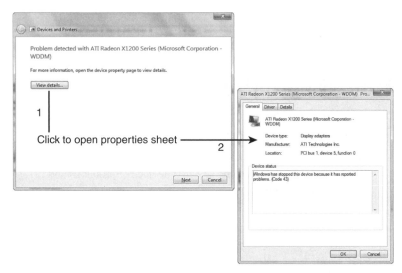

FIGURE 5.19   Troubleshooting problems with the display adapter.

3. Click **OK** to close the properties sheet.

4. Click **Next** to continue, and click **Close** on the next dialog.

Viewing Device Properties

Devices and Printers offer several levels of information about your device. When you select **Properties** from the right-click menu, the **General** tab displays information about the device or printer such as a manufacturer and model number, and the **Hardware** tab displays information about the device's hardware such as the device model number, device or printer type, device location, and device status.

Follow these steps to change settings:

1. Click the **Properties** button on the **Hardware** tab to display a separate multitabbed Properties dialog (see Figure 5.20).

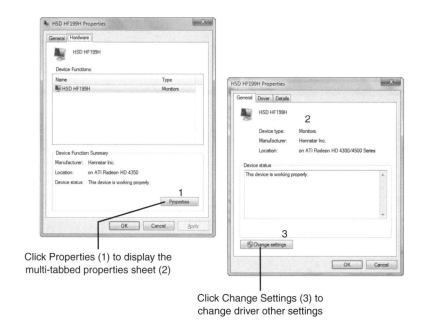

Click Properties (1) to display the
multi-tabbed properties sheet (2)

Click Change Settings (3) to
change driver other settings

FIGURE 5.20   Viewing properties for a display.

2. From this dialog, click the **Change Settings** button to open the
   Device Manager's properties sheet.

3. The Device Manager's properties sheet enables you to update the
   driver and view device status or error messages).

LESSON 6

Connecting to a Wireless Network

Checking Your System for Wireless Network Support

Before you can connect to a wireless network, you need to make sure that your computer is equipped for wireless networking and that your wireless network adapter is ready to work. A computer with a working wireless network adapter displays the Not Connected – Wireless Networks Are Available icon in the notification area when compatible wireless networks are nearby (see Figure 6.1). If you don't see this notification, your computer might not be equipped for wireless networking, or there might be a problem with your adapter.

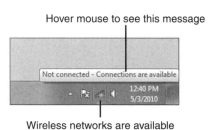

Hover mouse to see this message

Not connected - Connections are available

12:40 PM
5/3/2010

Wireless networks are available

FIGURE 6.1 This computer detects compatible wireless networks in range.

Follow these steps to find out whether your computer has a working wireless network adapter:

1. Click **Start**.

2. Click **Control Panel**.

3. Click **System and Security**.

4. Click **System**.

5. Click **Device Manager** (see Figure 6.2).

Click to open Device Manager

Path to System properties sheet

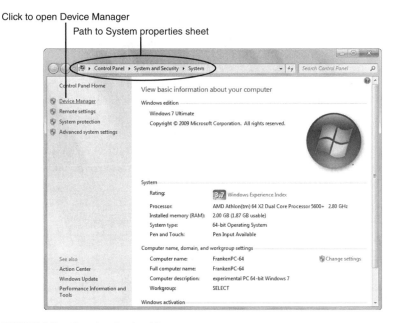

FIGURE 6.2   Opening Device Manager.

6. Expand the Network Adapters category to verify whether a wireless network adapter is available. Look for the Microsoft Virtual Wi-Fi Miniport Adapter; Windows 7 creates this virtual wireless adapter whenever a wireless network adapter is installed properly. If you don't see this adapter and you don't see an 802.11 or Wi-Fi adapter from another vendor, you need to add a wireless network adapter to your computer (see Figure 6.3).

Collapsed category

Expanded category

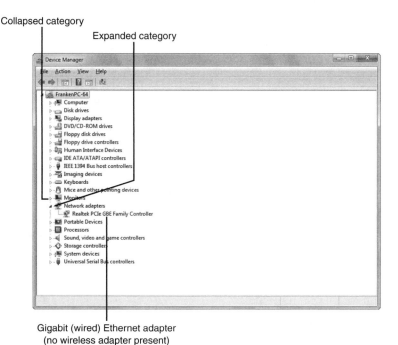

Gigabit (wired) Ethernet adapter
(no wireless adapter present)

FIGURE 6.3   A computer without a wireless network adapter.

7. After connecting a wireless adapter to your computer, it appears in Device Manager (see Figure 6.4).

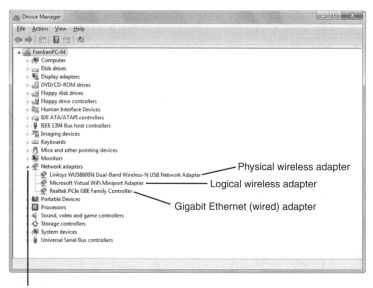

Expanded category

FIGURE 6.4   The same computer after a wireless network adapter is installed.

Troubleshooting Network Adapter Problems

If the wireless network adapter is marked with one of the following symbols, you need to solve a problem indicated by the symbol before you can use the adapter:

► A down arrow symbol indicates that the adapter is disabled and must be enabled before you can use it.

► A yellow triangle background indicates that the adapter has a problem that must be solved before you can use it.

Figure 6.5 shows examples of these symbols.

Device with problems

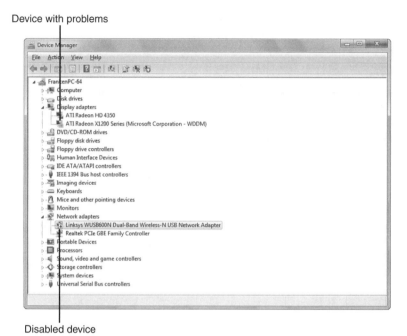

Disabled device

FIGURE 6.5   A computer with a disabled network adapter and a problem with its graphics adapter.

To enable a disabled adapter, use one of these methods:

▶ If the adapter is built into a notebook computer, there might be a button or a sliding switch on the top, on front of the computer, or along one of the laptop sides. This button or switch enables and disables the adapter. Press the button or slide the switch as appropriate.

▶ Right-click the adapter in Device Manager and select **Enable**. Follow the prompts to enable the adapter.

To enable a disabled adapter or to solve a problem with an adapter:

1. Double-click the **Adapter** icon to display the property sheet for the adapter,

2. Click the solution button on the **General** tab (see Figure 6.6).

Problem with adapter

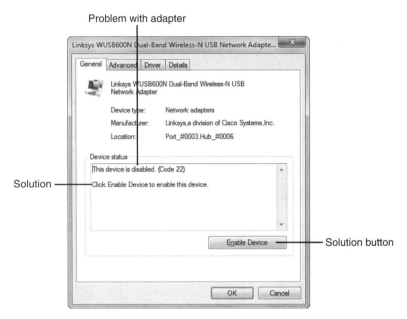

Solution

Solution button

FIGURE 6.6   Preparing to solve a problem with the wireless adapter.

When the adapter is working correctly, it appears as shown in Figure 6.4. At this point you can use your adapter to connect to a wireless network.

Viewing Available Wireless Networks

To view available wireless networks, click the Available Wireless Networks icon in the notification area of the taskbar (see Figure 6.7). Depending upon the networks available in your area, you might see one or more of the following types:

▶ **Open (Unsecured) Wireless Network**—Anyone can connect to this type of network because it doesn't require an encryption key (sometimes called a *password* or *passkey*). Because this connection is less secure than other types, it is marked with a yellow Windows Security Shield icon.

▶ **Secure Wireless Network**—You must provide the correct encryption key to connect to this type of network.

▶ **Other Network**—This network doesn't display its actual network name (SSID), so you must provide the SSID and encryption key when prompted.

▶ **Ad-Hoc Wireless Network**—Used mainly for sharing printers or all-in-one units between computers, it does not enable Internet access unless one of the computers in the network has a separate Internet connection using Internet Connection Sharing.

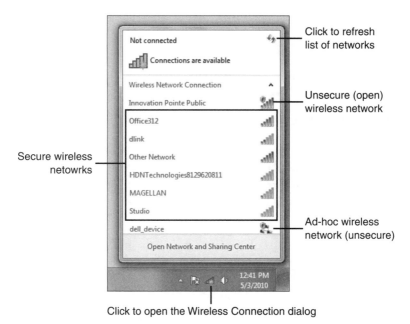

Click to open the Wireless Connection dialog

FIGURE 6.7   Opening the Available Wireless Networks dialog.

Follow these steps to learn more about each wireless network:

1. Hover your mouse over the network name to display information such as signal strength, security type, radio type, and SSID (see Figure 6.8).

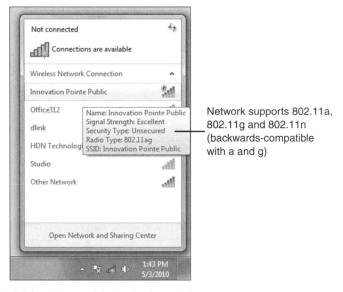

FIGURE 6.8   Viewing details about a wireless network.

2. Connections with four or more bars are listed as Excellent, whereas connections with three bars are listed as Good; connections with two bars are listed as Fair; and connections with one bar are listed as Poor. Ad-hoc connections don't list signal strength.

Connecting to a Wireless Network

Follow the appropriate procedure in the following sections to connect to a wireless network. With all network types, you can configure Windows 7 to connect automatically whenever the network is in range by clicking the **Connect Automatically** check box (see Figure 6.9). To start the connection process, click **Connect**.

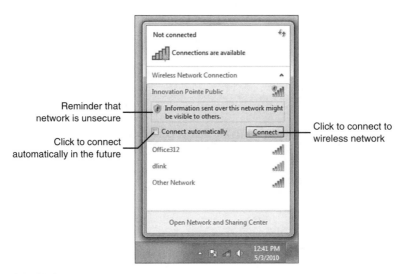

Reminder that network is unsecure

Click to connect automatically in the future

Click to connect to wireless network

FIGURE 6.9 Connecting to an unsecure wireless network.

Connecting to an Unsecured Wireless Network

After you click **Connect** follow these steps:

1. Windows 7 connects to the wireless network.

2. Messages display only if the connection fails.

Completing the Connection

After you connect to some wireless networks, you might see a notification (see Figure 6.10) indicating that you must open your web browser to complete the connection. Click the notification and provide the information required to set up your connection. You might need to install a security certificate or agree to terms of service before you can use the new connection.

Click to complete connection by providing input via your web browser

FIGURE 6.10   Prompt for additional information to complete a connection.

Connecting to a Secure Wireless Network

After you click **Connect** to connect to a secure wireless network, follow these steps:

1. Provide the security key required for the network (see Figure 6.11). By default, the security key text displays, but if you enter it in a location in which visible characters are a security risk, click the **Hide Characters** check box before you enter the key.

2. Click **OK**.

3. After the encryption key is verified, your connection is complete, and you can open your browser and use the Internet.

4. If you enter an incorrect security key, a **Security Key Mismatch** dialog appears, prompting you to enter the correct key.

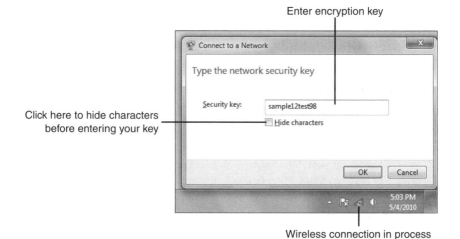

Enter encryption key

Click here to hide characters before entering your key

Wireless connection in process

FIGURE 6.11   Entering the security (encryption) key for a secure wireless network.

Connecting to Other Network

Some wireless networks do not broadcast their SSIDs. These wireless networks are listed as Other Network. To connect to this type of network, you must know the SSID and the security key (if used).

After you click **Connect** follow these steps:

1. Enter the SSID (wireless network name) when prompted (see Figure 6.12).

The SSID is case-sensitive

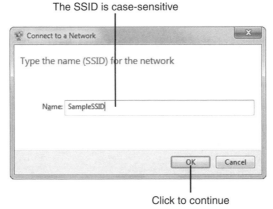

Click to continue

FIGURE 6.12   Entering the network name (SSID) for a nonbroadcast wireless network.

2. Enter the security key (if used; see Figure 6.11).

3. If this information is correct, your connection is complete. If not, a Windows Was Unable to Connect to *network name* error message appears.

Checking Current Connection Status

When you connect to a wireless network, a signal strength indicator appears in the notification area. To see the name of the network you're connected to, hover the mouse over the signal strength indicator (see Figure 6.13).

On some systems, you might need to click the up-arrow icon in the notification area to display the signal strength indicator.

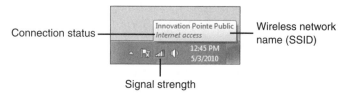

Connection status —— Wireless network name (SSID)

Signal strength

FIGURE 6.13 Viewing current connection information.

Disconnecting from the Current Network

To disconnect from the current network:

1. Click the signal strength indicator (see Figure 6.13) to display the current network and other wireless networks.

2. Click **Disconnect** (see Figure 6.14).

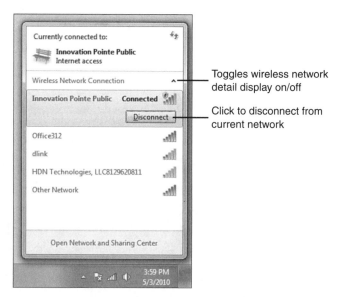

Toggles wireless network detail display on/off

Click to disconnect from current network

FIGURE 6.14 Disconnecting from a wireless network.

Configuring Network Location Settings

When you connect to a new wireless network, Windows 7 prompts you to select the correct network location setting with the dialog shown in Figure 6.15.

Also used for homegroups

Use for domain or workgroup networks

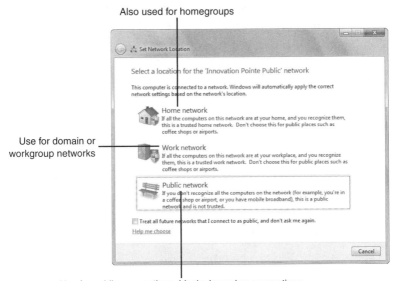

Use for public connections; blocks incoming connections

FIGURE 6.15   Choosing a network location.

Choose **Home Network** if you connected to a home network, such as a wireless router connected to your cable broadband or DSL service. Using Home as the network location also enables you to set up a homegroup with other Windows 7 computers on your home network (see Lesson 8, "Creating and Using a Homegroup," for details).

Choose **Work Network** to connect to a network at your office. Ask your network administrator for correct workgroup or domain settings; these can be changed through the System properties sheet. (Learn more about workgroup network settings in Lesson 9, "Connecting to Other Windows Computers.")

Choose **Public Network** to protect yourself from unwanted incoming traffic when you use unsecured networks in libraries, restaurants, hotels, and other public places. This setting also blocks network access to shared folders on your system.

Managing Wireless Connections

Windows 7 automatically stores wireless network connections. You can specify which connections to start, which to discard, what order to use them in; you can even store connection information for safekeeping or for use on another system by using Manage Wireless Networks.

Follow these steps to start Manage Wireless Networks:

1. Click **Start**.
2. Click **Control Panel**.
3. Click **View Network Status and Tasks**.
4. Click **Manage** Wireless Networks (see Figure 6.16).

Click to work with stored wireless network settings

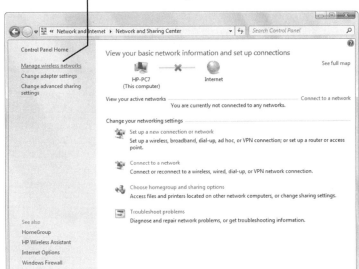

FIGURE 6.16   Starting Manage Wireless Networks from Network and Sharing Center.

Viewing the Properties for a Connection

The first time you use Manage Wireless Networks, all the wireless networks you have connected to are listed. To learn more about a particular network, right-click it and select **Properties** (see Figure 6.17).

Use the Connection tab (see Figure 6.18) to specify when to connect to the network (use it to change automatic connections to manual or vice versa) or to copy the network location to a USB flash drive for use on another computer. Use the Security tab (see Figure 6.18) to see and change (if need be) the security settings for the connection.

Displays properties for selected network

Displays properties for wireless adapter

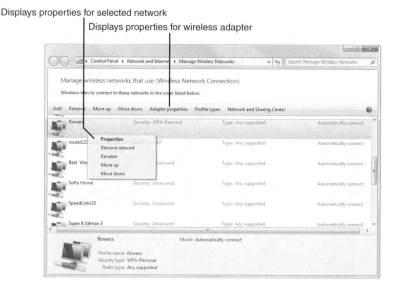

FIGURE 6.17   The Manage Wireless Networks dialog.

Change settings only if
network settings are
changed at the router or
wireless access point

Click to view characters
when possible; does not
always display characters

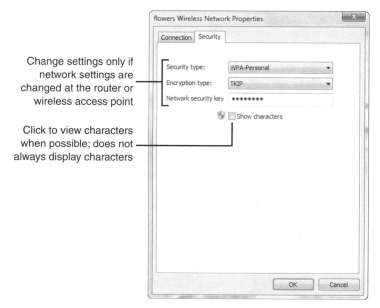

FIGURE 6.18   A wireless connection's Connection and Security tabs.

Copying Wireless Settings

To copy wireless settings for use on another computer, follow these steps:

1. Click the **Copy This Network Profile to a USB Flash Drive** link, as shown previously in Figure 6.18.

2. Connect a USB flash drive when prompted, and click **Next**. If your USB flash drive is not recognized, use a USB flash drive that does not install management software such as U3.

3. Note the instructions for transferring the settings to a new computer (see Figure 6.19), and click **Close**.

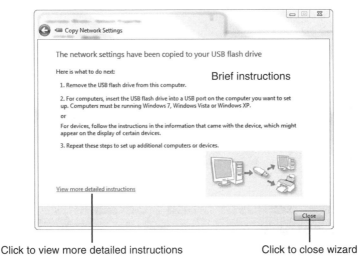

Click to view more detailed instructions   Click to close wizard

FIGURE 6.19   Completing the Copy Network Settings Wizard.

To use the USB drive to add a computer running Windows XP, Windows Vista, or Windows 7 to the same wireless network, follow these steps:

1. Plug the drive into the other computer.

2. Select **Connect to a Wireless Network** from the **AutoPlay** menu (see Figure 6.20).

Click to add this computer to the wireless network

FIGURE 6.20   Running Windows Connect Now from the AutoPlay menu.

3. Click **Yes** on the confirming dialog.

4. Click **OK** on the completion dialog.

Adding, Removing, and Reordering Connections

You can use several wireless network management options from either the right-click menu or from the menu bar. These include the following:

▶ **Remove (Remove Network)**—Removes the connection from the list. To reconnect to the network, you must connect manually and provide the correct settings.

▶ **Move Up**—Moves the selected network up the list. If more than one network configured for automatic connection is available at a particular time, Windows 7 connects to the one nearest the top of the list.

▶ **Move Down**—Moves the selected network down the list. Repeat Move Up or Move Down to place the network in the desired location on the list.

Closing Manage Wireless Networks

Click the **X** in the upper-right corner of the dialog to close Manage Wireless Networks.

LESSON 7

Browsing the Web Faster and More Securely with IE8

Starting Internet Explorer 8

You can start Internet Explorer 8 from the taskbar or from the Start menu. Internet Explorer 8 includes a jump list that offers several startup options. To choose from these options, follow this procedure:

1. Right-click the Internet Explorer 8 icon in the taskbar.

2. The jump list (see Figure 7.1) is divided into three sections.

FIGURE 7.1 A typical jump list for Internet Explorer 8.

3. To reopen a recently opened website, click it from the **Frequent** section.

4. To open InPrivate browsing or open a new tab, click the task desired from the **Tasks** section.

5. To open IE and go to its home page, click **Internet Explorer**.

6. To remove IE from the taskbar, click **Unpin This Program from Taskbar**.

7. After selecting an option to start IE, the Internet Explorer 8 window opens (see Figure 7.2).

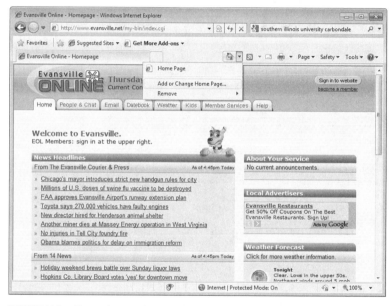

FIGURE 7.2   Preparing to change the default home page.

NOTE: To learn more about using jump lists, see Lesson 2, "Managing Your Desktop."

Changing Your Home Page

By default, Internet Explorer 8 uses MSN.com as its home page, but you can change the home page to any website you prefer. Here's how to make the change.

1. Enter the name or title of the website you want to use as your home page into the address bar.

2. Press **Enter**.

3. When the new home page appears, open the **Home Page** pull-down menu (see Figure 7.2).

4. Click **Add** or **Change Home Page**.

5. Click **Use This Website as Your Only Home Page**.

6. Click **Yes** (see Figure 7.3).

FIGURE 7.3   Making the current website the new home page.

7. The current website is now your home page.

Selecting Search Providers

When you start Internet Explorer 8 for the first time, Microsoft's default settings make Bing (formerly Windows Live Search) your default search provider. Here's how you can change to a different search provider:

1. Open the drop-down menu next to the Search window.

2. Click **Find More Providers** (see Figure 7.4).

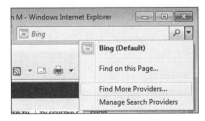

FIGURE 7.4   Starting the process of finding more search providers.

3. A list of providers displays. Click the **Add to Internet Explorer** button for the provider you want to add to your browser.

4. The Add Search Provider dialog appears. To add this provider but keep your current default, skip to Step 6.

5. If you want to make the new provider your default, click the **Make This My Default Search Provider** check box (see Figure 7.5).

FIGURE 7.5   Selecting Google as the new default search provider.

6. Click **Add**.

7. Your new search provider is now available. To add additional search providers, repeat Steps 1through 4 and 6.

TIP: If you don't see a listing for your preferred search provider, scroll to the bottom of the IE Add-Ons Gallery displayed in step 3 and click the **Create Your Own Search Provider** link. A new page opens; follow the instructions to set up your preferred search provider.

8. To switch between search providers, open the drop-down menu and select the search provider to use before entering search text.

Using Compatibility View

Some websites don't display properly in Internet Explorer 8. For example, note how the tabs in the website shown in Figure 7.6 are jumbled.

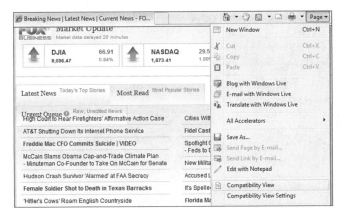

FIGURE 7.6   A website that doesn't properly display in Internet Explorer 8.

To enable websites that don't display properly to be usable in Internet Explorer 8, follow this procedure.

1. Click **Page** (see Figure 7.6).

2. Click **Compatibility View**.

3. The page displays in Compatibility view (see Figure 7.7).

FIGURE 7.7   Compatibility view enables the website to display properly in IE8.

Revisiting Websites More Quickly

Internet Explorer 8 now enables you to go to a website you've already visited more quickly by entering just a few characters in the website's URL or title, even if those characters are not at the start of the name. Here's how it works:

1. Enter part of the URL or title of a website you've already visited in the address bar.

2. Internet Explorer 8 displays matches from its website history (see Figure 7.8).

FIGURE 7.8   IE8 matches the text you enter in the address bar with URL or website titles in the website history it maintains.

3. Highlight a match and press **Enter**, or click the matching URL. IE8 opens the website.

Using InPrivate Browsing

Internet Explorer 8 normally stores the URL and title of each website you visit. However, if you want to keep your web-browsing activities confidential, you can use IE8s new InPrivate browsing feature to avoid storing this information. Here's how:

1. Open the **Safety** pull-down menu.

2. Click **InPrivate Browsing** (see Figure 7.9).

FIGURE 7.9   Opening the InPrivate browsing feature.

3. A new InPrivate browser window opens.

4. Enter the URL or website title you want to visit (see Figure 7.10).

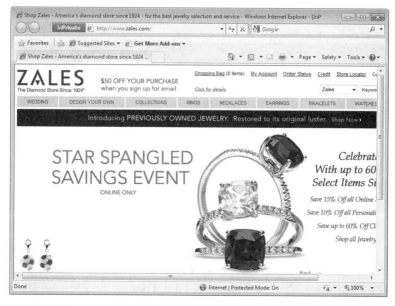

FIGURE 7.10   The InPrivate browser window.

5. When you finish with InPrivate browsing, close the InPrivate browser window.

IE8 does not add any website information visited with the InPrivate browsing feature to its regular history.

Creating and Using New Tabs

IE8 can display different Web pages in tabs. In most cases, it's better to open a new tab to display a Web page than to open a new browser window. Here's how to open a blank tab and use it for a different Web page:

1. Click the small empty tab next to an open tab.

2. A new tab opens (see Figure 7.11).

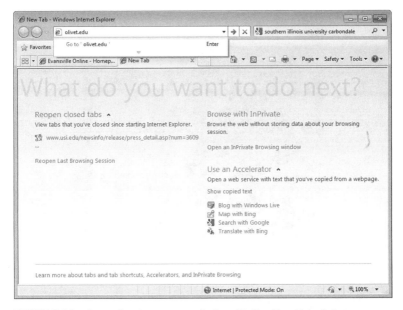

FIGURE 7.11   Preparing to open a website with the New Tab dialog.

3. To open a website, enter its text into the address bar and press **Enter**.

To open a new tab from a hyperlink in a website you are viewing, follow this procedure:

> NOTE: You can also reopen a closed tab or reopen the last browser session, open an InPrivate browsing window, or use accelerators from the New Tab dialog.

1. Right-click a link in an open website.

2. Select **Open in New Tab** (see Figure 7.12)

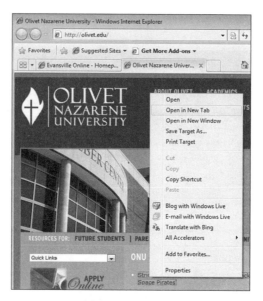

FIGURE 7.12   Preparing to open a website in a tab from the right-click menu.

3. The link opens in a new tab.

4. To view the tab's contents, click the new tab.

> NOTE: When you open other links from a tab, the original tab and the new tabs are highlighted with the same color so that you can see where the tabs were opened from.

Closing a Tab

Just as you can open new tabs, you can also close tabs you no longer need to use. Here's how.

1. Click a tab. It becomes the active tab.

2. Click the red **X** icon on the right side of the tab (see Figure 7.13).

FIGURE 7.13   Preparing to close a tab.

3. The tab closes.

4. Repeat Steps 1 through 3 as needed to close other tabs.

If you have more than one tab open, you can also close the current tab this way:

1. Click the red **X** icon at the upper-right corner of the browser window.

2. To close only the current tab, click **Close Current Tab** (see Figure 7.14).

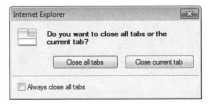

FIGURE 7.14   Closing the current tab only.

3. To close the browser and all tabs, click **Close All Tabs**.

Saving a Tab Group as a Favorite

If you open the same websites frequently, you might prefer to automate the process. By saving a group of tabs (also known as a *tab group*), you can open several tabs more quickly whenever you want. Here's how to do it:

1. Open a website you want as part of your tab group.

2. Create a new tab.

3. Open another website in that tab.

4. Repeat Steps 2 and 3 until all the tabs you want in your tab group are open.

5. Close any tabs that you don't want as part of your tab group.

6. Click **Favorites**.

7. Open the **Add to Favorites** pull-down menu.

8. Click **Add Current Tabs to Favorites** (see Figure 7.15).

FIGURE 7.15   Preparing to save a tab group.

9. Enter a folder name; your tab group will be stored in this folder.

10. By default, the tab group's folder is placed in the main Favorites folder. To select a different folder, open the **Create In** pull-down menu, and select where you want to place the folder.

11. Click **Add** (see Figure 7.16).

FIGURE 7.16   Providing a name and location for the tab group.

Making a Tab Group Your Home Page

By making a tab group your home page, you can automatically open your favorite websites when you start your browser or click the Home icon. Here's how to make it happen.

1. Create a tab group as discussed earlier in this lesson.

2. Open the **Home** pull-down menu.

3. Click **Add or Change Home Page**.

4. Click **Use the Current Tab Set as Your Home Page** (see Figure 7.17).

5. Click **Yes**.

FIGURE 7.17   Making the current tab group the home page.

Opening a Tab Group

After you create a tab group, you can open it whenever you want. Here's how it works.

1. Click **Favorites**.

2. Highlight the tab group.

3. Click the right arrow next to the tab group (see Figure 7.18).

FIGURE 7.18   Opening a tab group.

4. The tab group opens.

> NOTE: To open an individual website in a tab group, click the group name in Step 2. The tab group opens. Click the website you want to open.

LESSON 8

Creating and Using a Homegroup

Understanding Homegroups

Windows 7 includes an exciting new network technology called HomeGroup. Homegroups in Windows 7 enable you to securely share files of various types with other Windows 7 computers on your network while using a single password.

Homegroup networking is easy and secure, and it does not prevent you from sharing files, folders, and printers with other computers that don't use Windows 7 (see Lesson 9, "Connecting to Other Windows Computers," for details).

Setting the Network Location to Home

Windows 7 has three network location options available for any wired or wireless network connection: Home, Office, and Public. All computers in a homegroup must have their network location set as Home.

The first time you connect to a network, you are prompted to select the location (see Figure 8.1). Click **Home** to enable the computer to create or to be added to a homegroup. Click **Close** to finish the network location selection process.

If you don't remember your network location, you can open the Network and Sharing Center to find out:

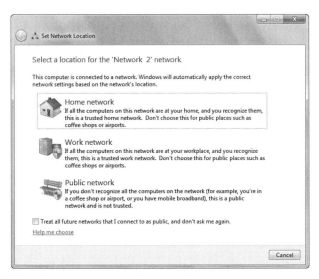

FIGURE 8.1   Preparing to select Home as the network location.

1. Click **Start**.

2. Click **Control Panel**.

3. Click the **View Network Status and Tasks** link in the Network and Internet category.

4. The network location is shown in the View Your Active Networks section of the dialog (see Figure 8.2). Note that the computer in Figure 8.2 has a location set as Work Network, making it ineligible to connect to a homegroup.

5. If you need to change the location (as with the computer in Figure 8.2), click the location type link (**Work Network, Public Network**) to display the dialog shown in Figure 8.1.

6. Click **Home** and then **Close**. Figure 8.3 shows the Network and Sharing Center for the same computer shown in Figure 8.2. This computer now features a HomeGroup status message of Available to Join because it is now located on a home network that already has a homegroup. If a homegroup is not present, the user is prompted to create one (see Figure 8.4).

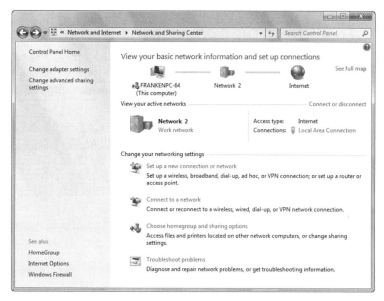

FIGURE 8.2 The Network and Sharing Center for a computer using a Work Network location.

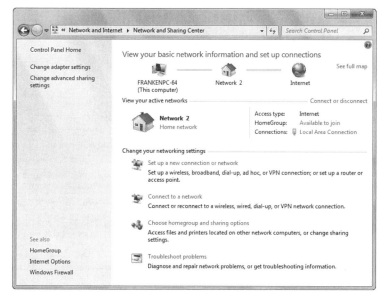

FIGURE 8.3 The Network and Sharing Center for a computer using a home network.

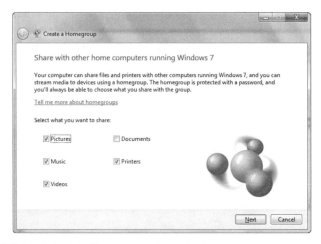

FIGURE 8.4   Selecting file types to share via the homegroup.

Each Windows 7 computer you want to add to a homegroup needs to have its location checked (and changed as needed) before you continue.

Creating a Homegroup

To create a homegroup:

1. Go to any Windows 7 computer on your network and click **Start**.

2. Click **Control Panel**.

3. Click the **Choose Homegroup and Sharing Options** link in the Network and Internet category.

4. Click **Create a Homegroup**.

5. Select the types of files to share. By default, any computer in the homegroup shares pictures, music, videos, and printers with other homegroup computers. You can also share documents or stop sharing other types of files (see Figure 8.4). Clear check boxes to stop sharing; click empty check boxes to start sharing.

6. Click **Next**.

7. Write down or print the password displayed (see Figure 8.5). You must use this password on other computers that will join the homegroup.

8. Click **Finish**.

FIGURE 8.5   Windows 7 generates a homegroup password.

TIP: To print the password, click the **Print Password and Instructions** link shown below the password window in Step 7.

Adding Other Windows 7 PCs to a Homegroup

As soon as a homegroup is created on a Windows 7 PC on your network, you can add other Windows 7 PCs to the homegroup. Follow these steps on each Windows 7 PC you want to add to the homegroup:

1. Click **Start**.

2. Click **Control Panel**.

3. Click the **Choose Homegroup and Sharing Options** link in the Network and Internet section.

4. Click **Join Now**.

5. Select the types of items you want to share (see Figure 8.4).

6. Click **Next**.

7. Enter the homegroup password from the computer used to create the homegroup (see Figure 8.6).

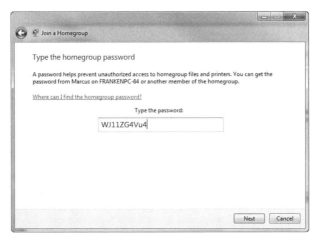

FIGURE 8.6   Entering the homegroup password.

CAUTION: Homegroup passwords are case-specific; in other words, you must enter the password exactly as shown, including the use of uppercase (capital) and lowercase (small) letters. If you misspell the password or use the wrong capitalization, you need to re-enter the password correctly before you can connect to the homegroup.

8. Click **Next**.

9. Click **Finish**. The Change Homegroup Settings dialog appears. You can make additional changes, or click **Cancel** to close the dialog.

NOTE: To learn more about the Change Homegroup Settings dialog, see "Changing Homegroup Settings" later in this lesson.

Using Files and Printers on Other Homegroup Computers

You can access any shared file or printer on other homegroup computers. To open files residing on other homegroup computers:

1. Click **Start**.

2. Click **Computer**.

3. Click **Homegroup** in the left pane.

4. Click the computer name that contains the file you want to use.

5. Navigate to the library or folder containing the file you want to open (see Figure 8.7).

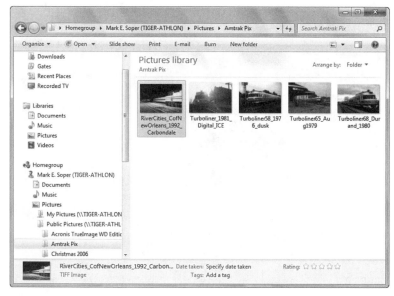

FIGURE 8.7 Selecting a file on a homegroup computer.

6. Double-click the file to open it.

To print with a printer located on a homegroup computer:

1. Open the print dialog.

2. Open the printer menu.

3. Select a printer on a homegroup computer (see Figure 8.8). Printers on other homegroup computers are listed as: *\\computername\printername*.

4. The first time you connect to the printer, you might be prompted to install printer drivers. Follow any prompts provided as needed.

5. Change printer settings as needed.

6. Click **Print**.

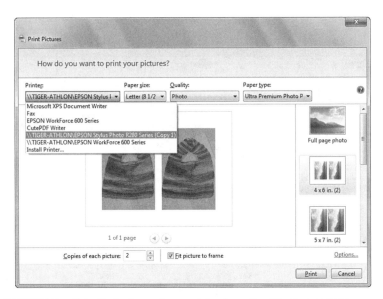

FIGURE 8.8   Selecting a homegroup printer from the Windows 7 Print Pictures Wizard.

Changing Sharing Settings

The normal settings for homegroup sharing provide read-only sharing of files in selected libraries; users can view and open, but can't change, add files, or delete files in a library. However, you might prefer to set up some libraries as read/write (enabling other users to save changes to existing files, delete files, or create new files and subfolders). This section shows you how to make these changes to your homegroup sharing settings.

To change sharing settings for specific libraries or folders:

1. Go to the computer whose sharing settings you want to change.

2. Click **Start**.

3. Click the username in the right pane of the Start menu.

4. Select the folder or library.

5. Click **Share With**.

6. Select the sharing option you want to use (see Figure 8.9):

- ▶ **Nobody**—Stops sharing the folder or library.

- ▶ **Homegroup (Read)**—Homegroup users can read folder contents but cannot change them.

- ▶ **Homegroup (Read/Write)**—Homegroup users can read, write, delete, and modify folder contents.

- ▶ **Specific people**—Choose specific users and specify their settings.

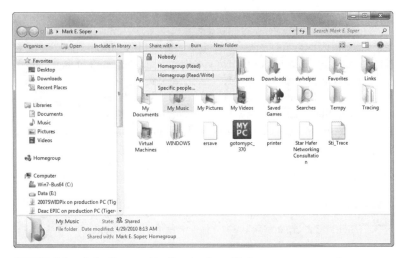

FIGURE 8.9   Selecting read/write sharing with homegroup users for a selected folder.

For example, if you want to have read/write access to your photo folders from other computers in the homegroup, select **My Pictures** in Step 4, and select **Homegroup (Read/Write)** inStep 6.

Changing Homegroup Settings

If you need to change settings for your homegroup, do the following:

1. Click **Start**.

2. Click **Computer**.

3. Right-click **Homegroup** in the left pane to display the menu shown in Figure 8.10.

4. Select **Change Homegroup Settings** to display the dialog shown in Figure 8.11.

The top of this dialog provides options for sharing libraries. The Share Media with Devices section controls media streaming. The Other Homegroup Actions section provides additional options.

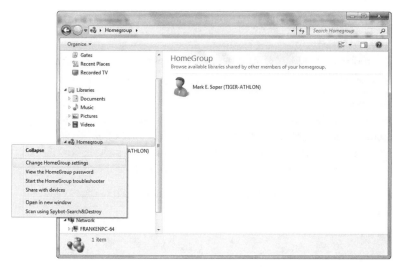

FIGURE 8.10 The right-click menu provides options for viewing and changing homegroup settings.

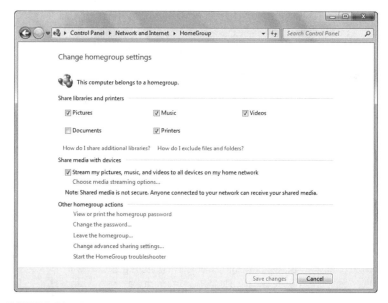

FIGURE 8.11 The Change Homegroup Settings dialog.

Changing Sharing and Media Streaming Settings

To stop sharing a library, clear the check box next to the library name. To share a library, click the empty check box next to the library name.

By default, pictures, music, and videos stream to other homegroup users through Windows Media Player or Windows Media Center. To disable media streaming, clear the **Stream My Pictures** check box. To specify which content streams, leave the **Stream My Pictures** check box checked, and click the **Choose Media Streaming Options** link.

With the Media Streaming Options dialog shown in Figure 8.12, you can specify which devices can access shared media.

FIGURE 8.12   The Media Streaming Options dialog.

NOTE: You can also open this dialog by selecting Share with Devices from the right-click Homegroup menu, as shown in Figure 8.10.

Hover the mouse over the row containing the device you want to manage connections for. Click **Remove** to remove the device from the list of devices permitted to receive streaming media. Click **Customize** to display the Customize Media Streaming Settings dialog shown in Figure 8.13. With this dialog, you can specify whether to stream all media, to restrict media by star ratings, or to restrict media by parental ratings.

FIGURE 8.13   The Customize Media Streaming Settings dialog.

> TIP: If you use star ratings to indicate your favorite media, enable the appropriate rating level so that other users see only media that meets or surpasses the ratings you specify. You can rate media by using Windows Media Center or Windows Media Player, or by adding ratings to the Details tab of the properties sheet for each media file.

Click **OK** to save changes made on either dialog.

Changing the Homegroup Password

Because all members of a homegroup use a single password to protect the homegroup, you might want to change the password from time to time, especially if you have temporarily added a friend's or houseguest's computer to the homegroup.

To change the password:

1. Make sure all computers on the homegroup are currently running and are not in sleep or hibernation mode.

2. On one computer, open the **Change Homegroup Settings** dialog and click the **Change the Password** link (see Figure 8.11).

3. The Change Your Homegroup Password dialog opens. Click **Change the Password**.

4. Enter a new password and click **Next** (see Figure 8.14).

FIGURE 8.14   Changing the homegroup password.

5. The new password displays. Be sure to print the new password or write it down, and then click **Finish**.

6. Go to all other computers in the homegroup and repeat Steps 2 through 5, using the same password you created in Step 4.

Troubleshooting a Homegroup

If you have problems connecting to other homegroup computers, select
the Start the HomeGroup Troubleshooter option, as shown in Figure 8.10
or 8.11.

1. From the opening screen, click **Next**.

2. Click **Troubleshoot Network Problems**.

3. Windows 7 might automatically apply fixes, or it might ask you
   one or more questions to help provide a solution (see Figure
   8.15).

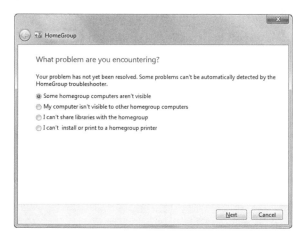

FIGURE 8.15   Provide answers when prompted to help the troubleshooter
solve your problem.

4. After Windows 7 applies suggested fixes, try to connect to other
   homegroup computers when prompted. If you succeed, click **Yes,
   the Problem Is Fixed**. If you still can't connect, click **No, the
   Problem Is Not Fixed** (see Figure 8.16).

5. If you selected **Yes** in step 4, Windows 7 displays the
   Troubleshooting Has Completed dialog and lists the problems it
   solved (see Figure 8.17). Click **Close**. If you selected **No** in Step
   4, follow the prompts to try other solutions.

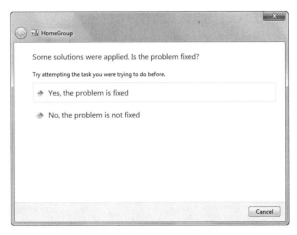

FIGURE 8.16 Try connecting again, and then click Yes or No as appropriate.

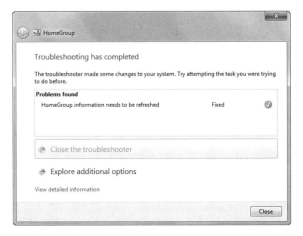

FIGURE 8.17 The Troubleshooting Has Completed dialog.

TIP: To learn more about specific troubleshooting steps Windows 7 performed, click the **View Detailed Information** link shown in Figure 8.17.

Leaving a Homegroup

It's not necessary to leave a homegroup when you move your computer from home to the office or from one location to the other: Other networks ignore homegroup settings, and Windows 7 will automatically connect you to your homegroup when you connect your computer to the network at home.

However, if you need to remove a computer from the homegroup, click the **Leave the Homegroup** link, as shown in Figure 8.11. This opens the Leave the Homegroup dialog, as shown in Figure 8.18. Click **Leave the Homegroup** and click **Finish**.

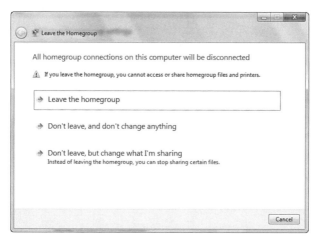

FIGURE 8.18   The Leave the Homegroup dialog.

To rejoin the homegroup, follow the procedure in the section "Adding Other Windows 7 PCs to a Homegroup."

LESSON 9

Connecting to Other Windows Computers

Viewing Computers Running Older Versions of Windows

When you connect your Windows 7 computer to a network that also has PCs running older versions of Windows, it might be necessary to make changes to the settings on some computers so that they can see each other to share folders and printers. Windows 7's Network folder is used to display all the computers visible on the network. Here's how to open it:

1. Click **Start**.

2. Click **Computer**.

3. Scroll down and click **Network**.

4. The computers that are visible and connected are listed in the right pane (see Figure 9.1).

> NOTE: You will see computers on your network if you set up your network location as Home or Work (see "Setting Up Network Discovery and Sharing with Network and Sharing Center" in this lesson for details). If your network location is set up as Public, you will see an information banner instead.

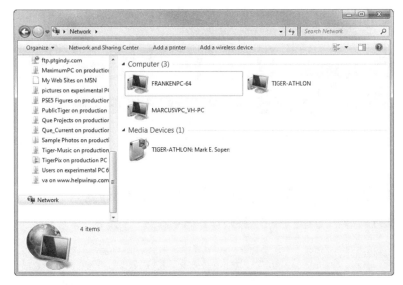

FIGURE 9.1   Viewing other computers on the network.

One of the computers listed in the right pane is your own computer. To determine the name of your computer:

1. Click **Start**.

2. Right-click **Computer**.

3. Select **Properties**.

4. The System properties sheet opens. The computer name is listed in the Computer Name, Domain, and Workgroup Settings section (see Figure 9.2).

Windows 7 connects automatically to other Windows 7 computers and Windows Vista computers. As soon as you connect your Windows 7 to a wired or wireless network that has computers running Windows Vista, those computers are visible on the network.

FIGURE 9.2   This computer is named FRANKENPC-64 and is part of the WORKGROUP workgroup.

Connecting to Windows XP–Based PCs

To make computers running Windows XP visible on the network to Windows 7 computers, the following changes might need to be made:

▶ **Configure the Windows 7 computer to use the same workgroup name (see Figure 9.2) as the Windows XP computer(s)**—By using the same workgroup name for all computers on the network, you enable Windows 7 computers to use shared resources on Windows XP computers, such as printers and folders.

▶ **Enable sharing on the Windows 7 computer**—This enables other computers on the network to use printers and folders on your computer according to what you decide to share.

Changing the Workgroup Name on the Windows 7 Computer

A workgroup is the traditional way of enabling computers to see each other on the network. If you cannot see Windows XP computers on the network, you need to change the workgroup name used by your Windows 7 computer to match the workgroup name used by the Windows XP computers. Here's how to find out the workgroup name:

1. Go to a Windows XP computer on the workgroup.

2. Click **Start**.

3. Right-click **My Computer**.

4. Select **Properties**. This displays the version of Windows XP in use and other information (see Figure 9.3).

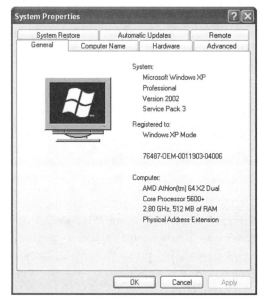

FIGURE 9.3   This computer runs Windows XP Service Pack 3.

5. Click the **Computer Name** tab (see Figure 9.4) to see the workgroup name.

FIGURE 9.4   This Windows XP computer is on a workgroup named MSHOME.

6. Click **OK** to close the dialog.

To configure your Windows 7 computer to connect to the workgroup:

1. Click **Start**.

2. Right-click **Computer**.

> NOTE: By default, Windows XP, Windows Vista, and Windows 7 are configured to use the workgroup name WORKGROUP. However, if you use the Home Networking Wizard in Windows XP to set up your home network with its default settings, the workgroup name is changed to MSHOME, as shown in Figure 9.4. You can also enter a custom workgroup name.

3. Select **Properties**.

4. Click **Change Settings** in the Computer Name, Domain, and Workgroup Settings section of the System properties sheet (see Figure 9.2).

5. The Computer Name tab opens. Click **Change**.

6. Click the **Workgroup** radio button.

7. Enter the name of your workgroup.

8. Click **OK** (see Figure 9.5).

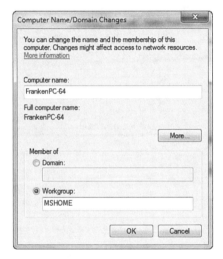

FIGURE 9.5   Changing to the MSHOME workgroup.

9. The Welcome to Workgroup dialog opens. Click **OK**.

10. The You Must Restart Your Computer to Apply These Changes dialog opens. Click **OK** to continue.

11. Click **Close** on the **Computer Name** tab of the System properties sheet.

12. Click **Restart Now**. When your computer restarts, other computers on the network can access your shared resources as soon as you specify what to share.

Setting Up Network Discovery and Sharing with Network and Sharing Center

To enable Windows XP computers to see your Windows 7 computer on the network, you might need to make changes to your current settings in Network and Sharing Center. Follow this procedure to check your settings:

1. Click **Start**.

2. Click **Network**.

3. Click **Network and Sharing Center**. The Network and Sharing Center dialog (see Figure 9.6) opens.

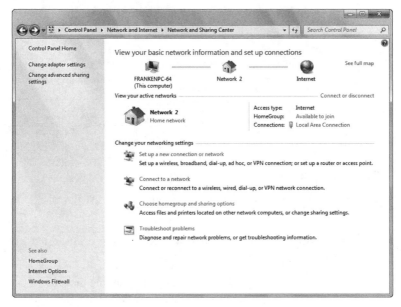

FIGURE 9.6   The Network and Sharing Center dialog.

4. To permit sharing, make sure your network type is set to **Home** (see Figure 9.6) or **Work**. If it is set to **Public**, change it to Home (if you have other Windows 7 computers and want to set up a homegroup) or **Work** (if you have a work network).

5. Click **Choose Homegroup and Sharing Options**. This opens the HomeGroup dialog in Figure 9.7.

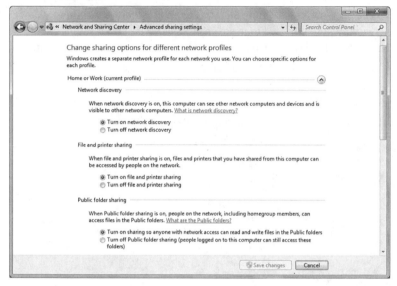

FIGURE 9.7   A portion of the Advanced Sharing Settings dialog.

6. Click Change Advanced Sharing Settings.

7. Make sure the following settings are configured as listed; make changes as needed:

   ▶ **Network Discovery: Turn On**—Turning this off makes your computer invisible on the network.

   ▶ **File and Printer Sharing: Turn On**—Turning this off prevents your computer from sharing any resources.

   ▶ **Public Folder Sharing: Turn On**—When turned on, permits read/write access to the Public folder on your computer from any computer on the network.

   ▶ **Password Protected Sharing: Turn Off**—If you turn this option on, you need to set up a user account on your computer for each user already on the network.

8. If you made any changes in Step 7, click **Save Changes**. Otherwise, click **Cancel** to close the dialog.

Opening Shared Folders

You can open the contents of a shared folder on the network with the following steps:

1. Click **Start**.

2. Click **Computer**.

3. Click **Network**.

4. Open the computer that contains the shared folder.

5. Navigate until you open the shared folder (see Figure 9.8).

FIGURE 9.8   Opening a shared folder on a Windows XP computer from a Windows 7 computer.

Adding a Shared Printer to Your Printer Menu

Before you can use a printer that is shared on the network, you need to add it to your list of printers. Here's how:

1. Click **Start**.

2. Click **Devices and Printers**.

3. Click **Add a Printer**.

> TIP: Double-click the computer and its folders to open them. Alternatively, click the computer or a folder once to select it, and then press the Enter key.

4. Click Add a Network, Wireless or Bluetooth Printer (see Figure 9.9).

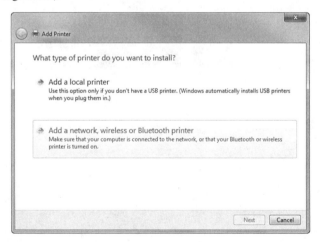

FIGURE 9.9 Choosing the option to add a shared printer.

5. Select the shared printer on another computer (see Figure 9.10).

6. Click **Next**.

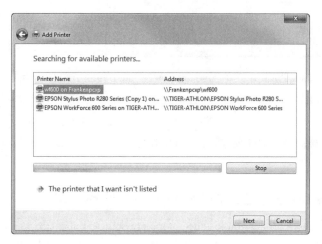

FIGURE 9.10   Selecting the shared printer.

7. After the printer is located, the Add Printer dialog confirms the printer has been installed. Click **Next**.

8. By default, the new printer is set as the default printer. To keep your current printer as the default, clear the check box, as shown in Figure 9.11.

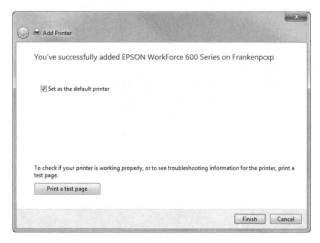

FIGURE 9.11   Preparing to test the shared printer.

> NOTE: If your computer has printers shared on the network, you
> see them listed as well (see Figure 9.10 for an example).

9. Click **Print a Test Page** and review the output from the shared
printer.

10. Click **Close** to close the Test Page print-confirming dialog.

11. Click **Finish** to close the Add Printer dialog.

Printing to a Shared Printer

If the shared printer you installed in the previous step is configured as the
default printer, all you need to do to use it is just click **Print from Your
Application**. However, if you set up the shared printer so that it is not the
default printer, you must choose it before you can use it for printing.
Here's how:

1. Open your application.

2. Open the **Print** menu.

3. Select the shared printer (see Figure 9.12).

4. Adjust other printer settings as needed.

5. Click **Print**.

> NOTE: A shared printer has a name with two backslashes (\\) at
> the start of the name: *computer**printername*.

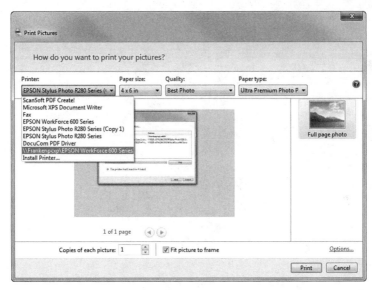

FIGURE 9.12   Selecting the shared printer while printing photos.

LESSON 10

Using Windows Backup

Understanding Windows Backup

Windows 7 includes Windows Backup, which enables you to perform two distinct types of backup at the same time:

▶ A disaster recovery image backup, which enables you to restore your entire system to a new hard disk in case of a hard disk or system failure

▶ File backup, which enables you to back up new and changed files

By creating a backup of your system and files, you can restore your system or individual files if your system or files are corrupted or deleted, or if you replace a file you need with a file you don't want to keep.

All versions of Windows 7 include Windows Backup, and you can back up both your system drive (C: drive) and additional internal and external hard disks connected to your system.

Using Windows Backup

To launch Windows Backup, follow these steps:

1. Click **Start**.

2. Click **Control Panel**.

3. Click **Back Up Your Computer** in the **System and Security** category.

4. The Backup and Restore dialog opens (see Figure 10.1).

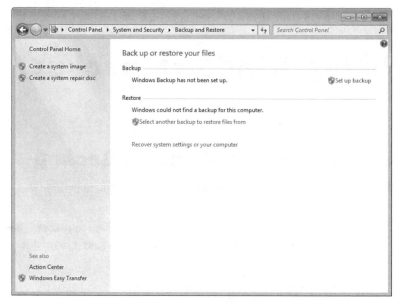

FIGURE 10.1   Windows Backup before your backup settings are configured.

The Windows Backup Interface

Figure 10.1 illustrates the Windows Backup interface when you run
Windows Backup for the first time. Windows Backup has two panes:

► The left pane is used to create a system image backup and a system repair disc.

► The right pane is used to configure Windows Backup, start
  Windows Backup, and run Windows Restore (used to restore files
  from a backup).

Running Your First Backup

Before you can use Windows Backup, you must set it up so that it knows
where to store the backups it creates and what you want to back up.
Here's how:

1. Connect the drive you want to use to store your backups to your system and turn it on.

> TIP: Although you can use a network connection (in Professional and Ultimate editions) or a different internal hard disk than the one used by Windows 7 for backup, I recommend an external hard disk connected to a USB 2.0 port, a FireWire port, an eSATA port, or a USB 3.0 port (listed from slowest to fastest). The drive's capacity should be at least 50percent larger than your system hard disk's total capacity. For example, if you have a computer with a 500GB hard disk, use a 750GB or larger backup drive.
>
> If you're not sure how large your computer's hard disk is, click Computer in the right pane of the Start menu. The capacity for your C: drive (used by Windows) is listed first.

2. Click **Set Up Backup**. This opens the Select Where You Want to Save Your Backup (see Figure 10.2) dialog.

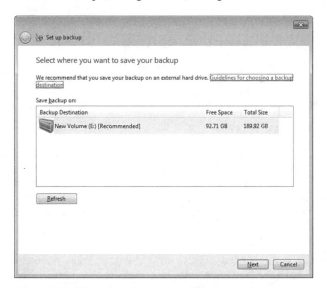

FIGURE 10.2   Selecting an external hard disk as the backup location.

3. Choose a location to store your backup. Select the external hard disk drive you connected in Step 1. If you did not connect an external drive, choose the drive you want to backup your data.

4. Click **Next**. The What Do You Want to Back Up dialog appears (see Figure 10.3).

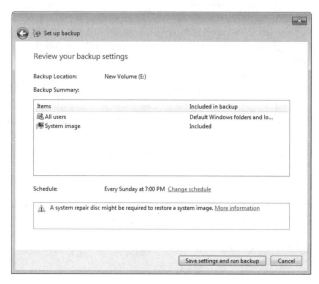

FIGURE 10.3   Reviewing the backup summary before creating your first backup.

5. Click **Let Windows Choose**.

6. Click **Next**.

NOTE: The Let Windows Choose option in Step 5 creates a system image and also backs up data files in libraries, default Windows folders, and your desktop. If you have added folders on external drives to one or more libraries (see Lesson 3, "Working with Libraries," for details), the contents of these folders will also be backed up.

If you use external hard disks to store photos, music, videos, or other information and have not added them to your libraries, click **Let Me Choose** in Step 5. This option selects all users' libraries on the computer, but you must select any additional locations to back up. For example, if you use Drive F: for digital photos and music, be sure to select that drive. Be certain that you don't forget anything!

7. Windows Backup displays a summary of what will be backed up and displays the backup schedule (see Figure 10.3). If you want to change the normal backup schedule, continue to Step 8. If you do not need to change the backup schedule, skip to Step 9.

8. To change the backup schedule, click **Change Schedule**. From the How Often Do You Want to Back Up? dialog (see Figure 10.4), choose frequency (daily, weekly, and monthly), day of the week, and time (1-hour increments starting at midnight). Click **OK** to close the dialog.

FIGURE 10.4   Changing the default backup schedule.

9. Click **Save Settings** and **Run Backup** to continue. Your first backup begins immediately.

> TIP: Because Windows 7 starts the first backup as soon as you click **Save Settings** and **Run Backup**, set up your backup at the end of your computing day. The first backup might take up to several hours to run, depending on the speed of your computer, your backup drive, and, most important, how much information will be backed up.

10. As the backup runs, a green progress bar appears in the Windows
Backup dialog (see Figure 10.5).

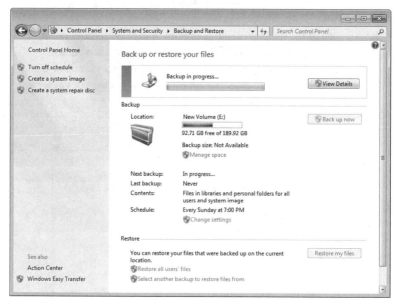

FIGURE 10.5   Running the first backup.

11. At the end of the backup, Windows Backup displays information
about the size of the backup, lists when the next scheduled backup will be run, and provides options for managing backups and
changing backup settings (see Figure 10.6).

NOTE: If you need to change the backup schedule, backup drive, or
what you back up, click **Change Settings** (see Figure 10.6).

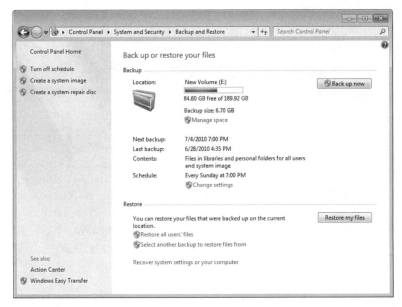

FIGURE 10.6   Windows Backup after completing a backup.

Creating a System Repair Disc

The Review Your Backup Settings dialog shown in Figure 10.3 states that a system repair disc might be needed to restore a system image. A system repair disc is a CD that you can use to start your computer if Windows 7 can't start, or if you need to restore your system image to a new or empty hard disk. If you have a Windows 7 disc, you can use it as a system repair disc, but if you don't, you should make a system repair disk. To make one, follow these steps:

1. In the left pane of Windows Backup (see Figure 10.6), click **Create a System Repair Disc**.

2. Insert a blank CD-R (recordable CD) disc into the CD or DVD drive listed in the Create a System Repair Disc dialog (see Figure 10.7).

3. Click **Create Disc**.

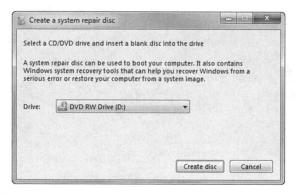

FIGURE 10.7   Creating a system repair disc.

4. After the disc is created, the disc is ejected from the drive. The Using the System Repair Disc dialog appears (see Figure 10.8).

FIGURE 10.8   Creating a system repair disc.

5. Label the disc.

6. Click **Close**.

7. Click **OK** to close the Create a System Repair Disc dialog.

CAUTION: Windows 7 is available in 32-bit and 64-bit editions. If you need to use a system repair disc, you must use a 32-bit repair disc on a 32-bit edition of Windows 7 and a 64-bit repair disc on a 64-bit edition of Windows 7.

> NOTE: To learn more about using the system repair disc, see "Windows 7 Backup and Restore, Part 2" at http://www.informit.com/articles/article.aspx?p=1400869 at InformIT.com.

Restoring Files and Testing Your Backup

After you make a backup, you should make sure that your backup files can be restored. If you want to test your backup, follow this procedure to create a folder you can use for testing.

1. Click the **Start** orb on the Windows desktop.

2. Click **your username** at the top of the right pane of the Start menu. This opens your user folders.

3. Click **New Folder**.

4. Type the name Backup Test and press the **Enter** key on the keyboard (see Figure 10.9).

FIGURE 10.9   Creating a test folder.

5. Close the window.

To restore your files from a backup, follow this procedure. In this example, you see how to restore the Sample Pictures folder to the folder you created in the previous step.

1. Start **Windows Backup**.

2. Click **Restore My Files**. The Restore Files dialog (shown in Figure 10.11) opens.

3. You can click **Search** to search for files to restore, **Browse for Files** to locate individual files to restore, or **Browse for Folders** to locate folders to restore. In this example, select **Browse for Folders**.

4. Navigate to the location containing the files or folder you want to restore. In this example, we want to restore the Sample Pictures folder (**Backup of C: > Users > Public > Pictures > Sample Pictures**).

5. Highlight the folder to restore.

6. Click **Add Folder** (see Figure 10.10).

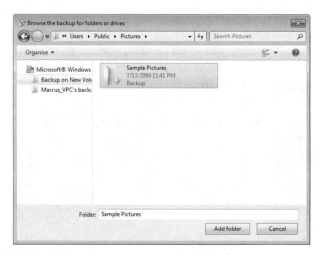

FIGURE 10.10   Selecting the Sample Pictures folder to restore.

7. The Restore Files dialog now lists the folder selected in Step 6 (see Figure 10.11). Click **Next** to restore this folder.

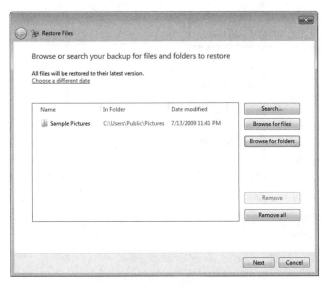

FIGURE 10.11   Preparing to restore the Sample Pictures folder.

NOTE: If you need to restore multiple folders or files, repeat Steps 3 through 6 until all folders or files have been selected.

8. To test your ability to restore files, click **In the Following Location**, and click **Browse** (shown later in Figure 10.13).

9. Browse to the location where you want to restore the files (the Backup Test folder created earlier) and click **OK** (see Figure 10.12).

10. Click **Restore** to restore your files (see Figure 10.13).

11. To open the folder containing the restored files, click the **View Restored Files** link. To close the **Restore Files** dialog, click **Finish**.

FIGURE 10.12   Selecting the Test Backup folder as the location for restored files.

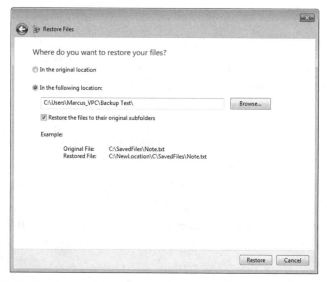

FIGURE 10.13   Restoring files to the Backup Test folder.

NOTE: If you are restoring deleted or lost files, click **In the Original Location** and click **Next** in Step 8, and then skip to Step 10.

LESSON 11

Using Action Center

Understanding Action Center

Previous versions of Windows report information about system security and maintenance in various locations in the Control Panel and elsewhere, such as Security Center, Windows Firewall, and Windows Backup. In Windows 7, Microsoft decided to create a single location for managing system security and maintenance settings: Action Center.

With Action Center, you can not only determine whether there are system security or maintenance issues to deal with, but you can also solve some problems directly from the Action Center dialog.

Starting Action Center

Action Center can be launched in two ways:

▶ From the System and Security category of the Control Panel

▶ From the notification area of the Windows desktop

To start Action Center from the Windows desktop:

1. Click the **Action Center flag** icon in the notification center.

2. Click **Open Action Center** (see Figure 11.1). Action Center opens (see Figure 11.2).

> TIP: To view Action Center messages, click the message listing in Step 2.
>
> To go directly to a reported problem in Step 2, click the problem listing.

FIGURE 11.1   Starting Action Center from the Windows desktop.

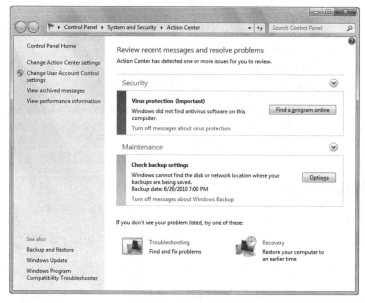

FIGURE 11.2   The Action Center dialog reporting security and maintenance issues.

The Action Center flag displays a red X icon if Action Center reports an important message and a yellow Exclamation Point (!) icon for other messages about your system.

The Action Center Interface

Action Center (see Figure 11.2) has two panes:

▶ The right pane is used to display messages and manage security and maintenance features in Windows 7.

▶ The left pane is used to manage Action Center settings and information about system reliability.

Responding to Action Center Messages

To respond to a message in Action Center, click the action button next to the message. As you can see from Figure 11.2, different messages display action buttons. One of the most common messages you see in Action Center is the message alerting you to the lack of an antivirus program; Windows 7 does not include an antivirus program. To deal with this message, perform the following steps:

1. Click **Find a Program Online**.

2. Your web browser opens the Windows 7: Consumer Security Software Providers Web page.

3. You can select a vendor and install its Windows 7 antivirus program, install a Windows 7–compatible antivirus program you have already downloaded, or install a Windows 7–compatible antivirus program you purchased.

4. After installing the antivirus program of your choice, Action Center no longer displays the message.

Similarly, if you click other action buttons and follow the prompts to a solution, Action Center will no longer prompt you when you reopen the program.

NOTE: To disable the display of Action Center messages, click the **Change Action Center Settings** link in the left pane of Action Center. Clear check boxes on the **Change Action Center Settings** dialog to disable security or maintenance messages.

To save messages for future review, click the **Archive This Message** link next to each message. To view these messages, click **View Archived Messages** in the left pane.

Viewing Information About Other Settings

To view information about other settings, click the down-arrow icon next to Security or Maintenance. Figure 11.3 illustrates the Security section of Action Center when there are no messages.

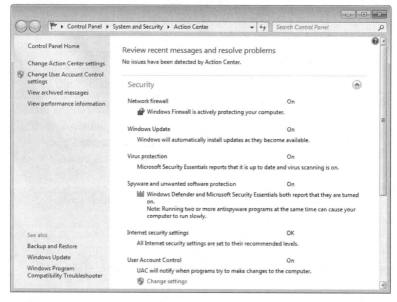

FIGURE 11.3   Security settings on a properly functioning system.

Table 11.1 lists the Security settings displayed in Action Center and how to change them if necessary.

TABLE 11.1   Security Settings Displayed in Action Center

Setting	Default	How to Change	Notes
Network firewall	On	Click **Start** > **Control Panel** > **System and Security** > **Windows Firewall**	Windows Firewall is included as part of Windows 7
Windows Update	Automatic updates –On	Click **Windows Update** link in left pane	—
Virus protection	Off	Install Windows 7–compatible antivirus software	—
Spyware and unwanted software protection	On	Click **Start** > type defen > click **Windows Defender**	Windows Defender is included as part of Windows 7
Internet Security Settings	OK	Click **Start** > **Control Panel** > **Network and Internet** > **Internet Options** > **Security** tab	—
User Account Control (UAC)	On	Click **Change Settings** link	—
Network Access Protection	Off	Enabled by network administrators	—

Figure 11.4 illustrates the Maintenance section of Action Center.

Table 11.2 lists the Maintenance settings displayed in Action Center and how to change them if necessary.

NOTE: Some features, such as User Account Control (see Figure 11.3) and Windows Backup (see Figure 11.4), can be changed directly from Action Center. However, in most cases, you can change settings from within Action Center only if Action Center displays a message.

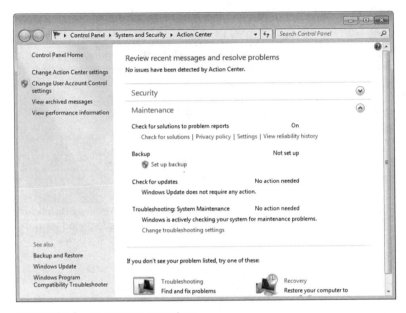

FIGURE 11.4   Maintenance settings.

TABLE 11.2   Maintenance Settings Displayed in Action Center

Setting	Default	How to Change	Notes
Check for Solutions to Problem Reports	On	Click **Change Action Center Settings** link in the left pane; click **Problem Report Settings**.	—
Backup	Not set up	Click **Set Up Backup** link.	Message changes after Backup is configured (see Lesson 10, "Using Windows Backup," for details).
Check for Updates	No action needed	Click **Windows Update** link in left pane.	No Action Needed means updates are downloaded and installed automatically.

TABLE 11.2   Maintenance Settings Displayed in Action Center

Setting	Default	How to Change	Notes
Troubleshooting System Maintenance	No action needed	Click **Change Troubleshooting Settings** link.	No Action Needed means Windows 7 is configured to check for problems automatically.

Launching Troubleshooters from Action Center

Windows 7 includes five categories of troubleshooters: Programs, Hardware and Sound, Network and Internet, Appearance and Personalization, and System and Security. In some cases, Windows 7 offers you a specific troubleshooter if you have a problem in any of these categories. Otherwise, if you click the **Troubleshooting** link at the bottom of Action Center, you open the Troubleshooting dialog, as shown in Figure 11.5.

To view all troubleshooters in a particular category, click the category name.

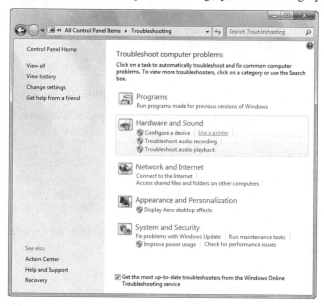

FIGURE 11.5   Windows 7 Troubleshooting page.

Troubleshooter Categories

Windows 7 troubleshooters are broken down like so:

▶ **Programs**—Offers troubleshooters for network, web browser, programs, printing, and media player

▶ **Hardware and Sound**—Offers troubleshooters for playing and recording audio, hardware devices, creating and playing optical media (CD, DVD, Blu-ray), network adapters, printing, media player, and TV tuner setup

▶ **Network and Internet**—Includes troubleshooters for Internet connections, sharing via folders and HomeGroup, and connections to other computers

▶ **Appearance and Personalization**—Includes troubleshooters for Windows Aero 3D desktop effects and display quality

▶ **System and Security**—Includes troubleshooters for Internet Explorer safety, system maintenance, performance, power settings, search and indexing, and Windows Update

Using Troubleshooters

Here's how to use these troubleshooters:

1. From Action Center, click the **Troubleshooting** link.

2. If the troubleshooter you want to run displays, click it. Otherwise, click a category, and then click the troubleshooter you want.

3. Click **Next** to continue.

4. The troubleshooter checks for problems.

5. Follow the prompts to help the troubleshooter solve your problems.

6. If the troubleshooter cannot solve your problem, it provides alternative solutions.

For example, if you have problems running a program made for older versions of Windows in Windows 7, here's how to use the program troubleshooter:

1. Click **Run Programs Made for Previous Versions of Windows**.

2. Click **Next**.

3. Select the program that isn't running properly.

4. Click **Next**.

5. To use the recommended settings, click **Try Recommended Settings**.

6. Click **Next**.

7. The troubleshooter lists the compatibility settings it selected. Click **Start the Program**.

8. After running the program, close it and return to the troubleshooter.

9. Click **Next**.

10. If the program runs correctly, click **Yes**, Save These Settings for This Program. If the program doesn't work, click **No, Try Again Using Different Settings**. If you have tried several different settings and the program still won't work, click **No, Report the Problem to Microsoft and Check Online for a Solution**. (see Figure 11.6).

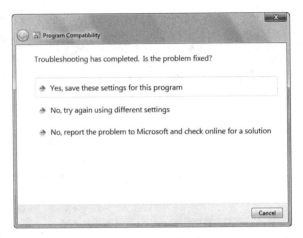

FIGURE 11.6   Completing the program troubleshooter.

NOTE: If the **Try Recommended Settings** option doesn't work, click **Troubleshoot Program** in Step 5 and choose the appropriate answers as prompted. Windows 7 uses the answers you post to select specific program compatibility settings.

Index

Internet Explorer 8
> Compatibility view, 147
> home page, changing, 144-145
> InPrivate Browsing, 149-150
> revisiting websites more quickly, 148
> search providers, selecting, 145-146
> starting, 143-144
> tabs
>> *closing, 152-153*
>> *creating, 150*
>> *making a tab group your home page, 155*
>> *opening tab groups, 156-157*
>> *opening websites from, 151-152*
>> *saving as Favorites, 154-155*

J-K

jump lists
> defined, 29
> examples, 30-29
> explained, 21-23
> options, 25-26
> pinning/unpinning items on, 23-25, 31

Keyboard Settings option (Devices and Printers applet), 106

L

Large Icons view, 56
launching. *See* starting

Leave the Homegroup dialog, 175
leaving homegroups, 175
Length view, 55
libraries
> columns
>> *adding/removing, 60-64*
>> *changing column width and order, 64-65*
>> *grouping, 65-66*
> explained, 49
> folders
>> *adding, 50-52, 69*
>> *sorting, 59-60*
> managing, 68-70
> viewing, 49-58
> views, 52-58
>> *Album view, 54*
>> *Arranged by Tag view, 53*
>> *Date Modified view, 53*
>> *Details view, 57-58*
>> *Extra Large Icons view, 56*
>> *Large Icons view, 56*
>> *Length view, 55*
>> *List view, 57*
>> *Medium Icons view, 56*
>> *Tiles view, 57*
> in Windows Media Center, 94-96
Library Location Is dialog, 52
List view, 57
lists
> jump lists
>> *defined, 29*
>> *examples, 30-29*
>> *explained, 21-23*

movies, playing in Windows Media Center, 96-98

moving network connections, 140-141

multifunction devices, 117

managing, 116

Multiple Displays menu, 45

N

navigating

Devices and Printers applet, 101-102

Windows Media Center, 93-94

Network and Sharing Center dialog, 183

network discovery and sharing, setting up, 183-185

Network Settings option (Devices and Printers applet), 105

networks

connecting to Windows XP-based PCs, 179-185

changing workgroup name on Windows 7 computer, 180-182

network discovery and sharing, 183-185

homegroups. *See* homegroups

shared folders, opening, 185

shared printers

adding, 186-188

printing to, 188

viewing computers running older versions of Windows, 177-179

wireless. *See* wireless networks

O

opening

shared folders, 185

Start menu, 7-8

tab groups, 156-157

websites from tabs, 151-152

Optimize This Library For menu, 69

P

Password Reset Disk

creating, 16-19

logging in with, 19-21

Password Reset Wizard, 19-21

passwords

for homegroups, 171-172

Password Reset Disk

creating, 16-19

logging in with, 19-21

viewing password hints, 6-7

Photo Viewer. *See* Windows Photo Viewer

photos. *See also* Windows Photo Viewer

emailing, 79-81

magnification, 74-75

printing, 81-83

rotating, 74-75

viewing in slide show, 77

viewing in Windows Media Center, 98-99

pinning

items on taskbar, 31-32

items onto jump lists, 23-25, 31

Sams**TeachYourself**

from Sams Publishing

Sams **Teach Yourself in 10 Minutes** offers straightforward, practical answers for fast results.

These small books of 250 pages or less offer tips that point out shortcuts and solutions, cautions that help you avoid common pitfalls, and notes that explain additional concepts and provide additional information. By working through the 10-minute lessons, you learn everything you need to know quickly and easily!

When you only have time for the answers, Sams Teach Yourself books are your best solution.

Visit **informit.com/samsteachyourself** for a complete listing of the products available.

 FREE Online Edition

Your purchase of **Sams Teach Yourself Microsoft Windows 7 in 10 Minutes** includes access to a free online edition for 45 days through the Safari Books Online subscription service. Nearly every Sams book is available online through Safari Books Online, along with more than 5,000 other technical books and videos from publishers such as Addison-Wesley Professional, Cisco Press, Exam Cram, IBM Press, O'Reilly, Prentice Hall, and Que.

SAFARI BOOKS ONLINE allows you to search for a specific answer, cut and paste code, download chapters, and stay current with emerging technologies.

Activate your FREE Online Edition at www.informit.com/safarifree

> **STEP 1:** Enter the coupon code: SXMFQGA.

> **STEP 2:** New Safari users, complete the brief registration form. Safari subscribers, just log in.

If you have difficulty registering on Safari or accessing the online edition, please e-mail customer-service@safaribooksonline.com